Genesis

The People's Bible Commentary

GENESIS

Henry Wansbrough

The Bible Reading Fellowship
OPENING THE BIBLE

Text copyright © Henry Wansbrough 1996

The author asserts the moral right to be
identified as the author of this work.

Published by
The Bible Reading Fellowship
Peter's Way, Sandy Lane West
Oxford OX4 5HG
ISBN 0 7459 2821 8
Albatross Books Pty Ltd
PO Box 320, Sutherland
NSW 2232, Australia
ISBN 0 7324 1546 2

First edition 1996
10 9 8 7 6 5 4 3 2 1 0

Acknowledgments
Unless otherwise stated, scripture quotations
are taken from the New Jerusalem Bible
copyright © 1985 by Darton, Longman &
Todd Ltd and Doubleday & Company Inc.

A catalogue record for this book is
available from the British Library.

Printed and bound in Great Britain
by Cox and Wyman Limited, Reading

Contents

Introduction

This first volume in the series offers a commentary for reflective reading on the first book of the Bible. In order to situate and appreciate the wonder of the revelation of God which is contained in the Book of Genesis the briefest of sketches of its history will be helpful.

We must work backwards. The book was completed, ready for what would nowadays be 'publication', only after the Babylonian Exile, some 400 years before Christ. It then received only a few finishing touches, and the vast majority of the stories and traditions it contains go back many centuries before that.

Part of the divine guidance which so painstakingly formed and guarded God's people consisted in enabling them to preserve these traditions intact, as they were handed down with astonishingly correct detail. Many of these details would have made no sense to those who faithfully told the stories generation after generation. It is only through modern archaeological discoveries that we can know that many details reflect ancient historical situations or law codes long outmoded.

At the same time the historically-minded reader may see some reflection of the periods through which these traditions passed. The accounts of the relationship of the world to God and the origins of humanity in Genesis 1–11 reached pretty well their final form during the Babylonian Exile (during the seventy years after the Sack of Jerusalem in 597). In these expressions of the age-old theology of Israel may be traced the struggles of the exiles against the many gods of Babylon.

The stories about Abraham, Isaac, Jacob and their families in Genesis 12–36 were handed down in three often overlapping streams of tradition. (The story of Joseph in Genesis 37–50 is much more unified, and must be seen as a coherent whole.) These are sometimes still recognizable from their different tone and emphasis.

The oldest stream of tradition is known as the Yahwist account, because it uses the name 'Yahweh' for God, although the actual name was revealed to Moses only later. It is a lively, warm and often humorous account, which obviously takes delight in human motives and characters. From the special interest in events in the southern part of the country one may guess that this stream of tradition was handed down in the southern region, Judah.

The other principal stream of tradition is called the Elohistic tradition (the name used for God is 'Elohim'). This is more concerned with details of morality. Its place names suggest that it stems from the northern part of the country, Israel.

A third stream is known as the Priestly writer, since this shows an overwhelming interest in details of cult and genealogies.

These three different approaches enrich and give variety to the history of God's people. The minor variations between the accounts are typical of folk-history handed down by word of mouth. They give the reader a sense of the loving care of God for his people all through the millennium and a half between Abraham and the final 'publication' of the book.

1 The creation

Origins

Every culture has stories about its origins. If you know how something came to be, you are well on the way to understanding what it is. The Greek myths of Prometheus or Pandora's Box are classic examples. In this century, Rudyard Kipling's *Just So Stories* fascinate generations of children by 'explaining' how the leopard got its spots or why the cat walks by itself.

The Hebrews were fascinated by origins too, and many of the stories in the Bible are geared to explaining how features of life or landscape came to be. By so doing the story-teller explains their significance too. So the purpose of the first eleven chapters of Genesis, before the story of Abraham begins, is to explain the basic structure of things as they are.

History has importance only in so far as it explains the present. The early stories of Genesis are important in that they explain the basic structure of the world and enable us to understand ourselves better. And for the Hebrew the basic structure of the world and the human person has sense only in relationship to God.

The first story of creation

Obviously there are two stories of creation, one after the other, in the Bible. The first has wider horizons, embracing the whole universe, sun, moon and stars. The second concentrates on Adam in his garden. The first is carefully and minutely ordered, built on the scaffolding of seven days, like the Hebrew week. The author wants to show that this structure of seven days, ending with God's own day of rest, is part of the basic structure of the universe.

What really gives the clue to the purpose of the story is the order within the days. The story is attempting to represent not the order in which things happened but their scientific structure. Sun and moon are not created until the fourth day, and it is hard to envisage what can be meant by a day without sun and moon. The gap between the creation of light and darkness on the first day and sun and moon on the fourth is also odd. The pieces fit perfectly together when the real principle of order appears: it is a scientific division, not a time-sequence. 1. The basic framework of things: light and darkness. 2. Fixed things: heavens above, waters beneath, land and its fixed contents (plants). 3. Mobile things: stars in the heavens, fish in the seas, animals on the earth—and finally human beings.

The Babylonian factor

Like so much of the older part of the Bible, the account took its detailed shape during the Babylonian Exile. It was no novelty to Israel that the Lord God was responsible for their existence, both in the first place and in continuity. But in Babylon they were confronted with stories and myths about the gods who formed the cosmos.

Against these they reacted, using the same symbols but forming a wholly different picture. The Babylonian gods squabbled among themselves. Marduk, the chief god, formed the world by splitting a goddess and hanging her up 'like a fish in the drying-yards' (a kipper being smoked, in our terminology). He formed man from the blood of a goddess to serve the gods by feeding them on the delicious smell of his sacrifices. How much more dignified, how much more caring is the God of the biblical stories! No squabbling, no need for any previous material, no dismembered gods. Sun, moon and stars are not gods, nor even seats of the gods, but mere timing-devices to indicate times and festivals sacred to God.

The human being is no lackey to the gods, but is created (after a thoughtful pause) in the image and likeness of God, to the awesome function of being God's own representative to all the other creatures, not dominating them in an arbitrary manner, but caring for them as God cares for them. Bubbling through the whole account is the constant blessing of God and the constant refrain, 'and God saw that it was good'. This is a positive world. We are beginning not a horror story but an account of God's blessing.

PRAYER

Lord God, without effort you created all things good and blessed them for the future. Grant us to accept your blessing and to appreciate our daunting task to be your representatives to all creation.

2 The Garden of Eden

The Garden

The second story of origins works on a less grand scale than the first. All the focus is on the Garden of Delight, for that is what 'Eden' means in the story. Originally the 'garden *in Eden*' may have indicated its geographical location, but more important is the link to a similar Hebrew word which means 'delight'. It is a sort of Never-Never Land, a paradise for which we now yearn, where everything is as it should be. This is indicated by the abundance of water.

In a hot, dry, sandy terrain, where much of the country is desert, incapable of growing anything, the gift of moisture is mouth-watering. Bring water to this arid land, even in drips, and immediately vegetation springs up. In a climate where dehydration sets in quickly, the mouth gets drier and drier, the body stickier and stickier, the sight of a stream of water makes the heart leap. In this garden water flowed out of the earth, and in such quantity that it flowed out into four great rivers. This is enough to conjure up life, vegetation, fertility, richness, abundance. In this garden of delights the Man is not entirely carefree. The limits to his freedom of action are indicated by the prohibition of eating of the tree of good and evil. The very name of the tree indicates a moral restriction for him: the shape and constitution of his environment is such that not everything is right for him. The way this prohibition is imposed appears at first sight to be arbitrary: God simply imposes it.

This is, however, a pictorial way of showing that there are limits outside of the individual which the individual may not transgress, and that this is a condition of his very existence. He cannot decide for himself what is good and what is evil. The structure of good and evil is an unchangeable part of the fabric of his world.

My family and other animals

Once this moral structure has been outlined, the story moves on to social relationships, first the living world in general, but leading up to the climax of human companionship. God forms the birds and animals, but in bringing them to the Man to be named, God gives the Man a part in his creation. The importance of this element is shown by the fact that both creation stories insist upon it.

In this story the Man gives the animals their nature by naming them, for the name and the nature are complementary. It also gives the Man a certain proprietary right over the animals he has helped to form. If you can't describe something or give it a name, you have little concept of it or power over it; the ability to grasp it in this way gives a power over the object.

But in both stories, the Man's share in God's creative power does not imply that he has arbitrary power to use the birds and animals just as he wishes. He also has responsibility towards them, to show to them the care and love which God shows to him.

We have become much more aware in recent years of this responsibility of human beings to their environment, largely by contrast to the uncaring abuse of creation which modern science and technology have made possible; but the seeds of this divine duty are already planted in this story of creation.

The lovely climax of the account comes in the creation of human companionship between man and woman. This is the climax of God's loving care. The story, of course, concentrates on the Man, and for the majority of the story the Man stands for the whole of the human race. The completion and corrective comes at the end, for the Woman is no servant or object for the Man. This is stressed in every possible way.

Without the Woman the Man is lacking a helper and companion. The Woman shares the material, the flesh and bones of the Man. He greets her with delight ('at last'!), proclaiming her equality in his little poem. This is all the more remarkable in the context of ancient civilizations where the equality of the sexes and the inherent dignity of women could not be taken for granted. Yet this story analyses it as part of the fabric of the human world. They stand before each other, proud and equal in their nakedness, without shame or fear.

PRAYER

Creator of the world, give me reverence for all you have given to us. Help me to appreciate my dignity as your representative. Enable me to share your care and respect for your creation, and especially for other people and their diversity. Help me to treasure especially the unique bond and blend between man and woman.

3 The Fall

The subtle serpent

The story of the Fall is beautifully told. The snake persuades the woman with great subtlety, carefully flattering her, allowing her a correction here and there, appealing to her curiosity and pride. By the time she comes actually to eat the fruit, she must have been feeling really pleased with herself. The world is smiling. She is definitely the superior, and passes the fruit on to her husband. But as soon as they have eaten, everything changes: they feel remorse, fear and desolation.

The partners cling together to provide each other with some sort of support. The man blames the woman, the woman blames the snake. Their nakedness is nothing to do with sexual attraction; it is the extreme of defencelessness and shame, as they stand there naked for all to see. Once, they could hold their heads high and accept their bodies as the glorious expression of God's creative act. Now they want only to hide, hide from God, hide from anything. But they have nothing to hide behind, not even clothes.

Then follows the sentence of God, and the world as we know it comes into being. For the woman there will be two sorrows: travail in childbirth and a position of subordination to male dominance. As for man, he has the drudgery of earning his bread (in a world where this was left to men—nowadays the drudgery spreads equally to women too, and women get the worst of both punishments!). The snake is punished for its part by being changed from a great, fiery heraldic dragon (for the Hebrew word can mean that as well) into an enlarged worm, crawling on its belly. But the situation does not stop there. A promise is given that evil will not for ever triumph: the seed of the woman will succeed in damaging the tempter, though not without cost.

The story of human failure

The story as we have it was probably written down in exile in Babylon after 586BC. Many of the images used—the tree of life, the tempting snake, the loss of innocence and harmony—occur also in Babylonian stories of the time. The inspired thinkers of Israel took these and wove them into their own story of human relationships with God and with evil. For us today it becomes a picture of human failure at any time.

In Adam (and *adam* is simply the Hebrew word for 'man') and Eve we can see ourselves, self-confident, sure of our own powers, determined to make our own decisions and get pushed around by no one, not even by God, aiming to live for ever by our own capacities. But then the shame, confusion and humiliation when things do go wrong!

What is the sin portrayed? Some have thought that it is a sexual sin. While there may be elements which can be interpreted as sexual, the sin can also be understood more widely, as a sin of pride and independence: the woman is determined not to be bound by any divine command, but to be her own judge; she will be like God, deciding for herself what is good and evil. That, basically, is the form of any sin: we make our own decision, pretending to ourselves that there is no law beyond ourselves, that any restrictions do not apply in our case. It is only afterwards that conscience reasserts itself with explosive vigour.

A thread of hope

The encouraging aspect of the story is its controlled optimism. We have already seen that God created the world good. Now human beings do their best to shatter the divine harmony of creation. But hidden amid the dire consequences lurks the promise that all is not lost, that good will triumph in the end. Some human philosophies, some historical traditions are full of gloom and despair, seeing no good in the world and the circumstances around us.

The tradition which comes from Israel is a positive and hopeful one. Pessimism and despair have no place in it. Recognition of evil and failure, yes, but never their final triumph. In the course of the revelation in the Bible it becomes gradually clearer how good must triumph despite our constant failures. History is a record of human incompetence and conquest of evil. This discord finds its resolution in the supreme act of human generosity by the God who becomes human.

PRAYER

Father, hold us firm in your hands. Keep us always aware that without you we cannot fulfil what we promise, but in you we may always be confident and secure.

4 Cain and Abel

The story of Cain and Abel as it now exists suggests a much wider world than the second generation of human beings: in his punishment after the murder, Cain can wander over the earth and come in contact with other peoples who may want to kill him. The two sacrifices which start the jealousy already suggest quite a development of sacrifice, approaching the later system by its selection of the firstborn and some of the fat.

An agricultural way of life, tilling the soil, is also far advanced in the development of human husbandry. The transition to flocks and agriculture occurred hardly 10,000 years ago. It may therefore be an independent story of the origin of evil, not organically connected with the generation after Adam and Eve. It could reflect and personify the opposition between two different systems of husbandry.

This story puts jealousy as the basic sin, instead of the pride and self-will shown in the story of Adam and Eve. As it stands now, however, the story shows the development of disorder in human relations. Original sin means that, once sin has been committed, there is a knock-on effect: if I tyrannize my weaker neighbour, that neighbour will find another weaker person on whom to take out the frustration caused. Disorder entered into human relations by the sin of Adam. The loss of innocence signified by the shame at their nakedness is translated into loss of confidence, a fear of being judged inferior, and a need to be self-assertive.

God's two questions play the part of the conscience. First, they just raise the question, 'Where is your brother?', when the guilty party would like to forget all about it. Then, 'What have you done?' to induce the guilty to face the quality of his action. Cain's reaction, too, is typical of the guilty conscience, aggressive and defensive, at first trying to deny responsibility. Only when sentence of alienation has been passed—he must flee from his crime—does he accept the blame and turn to begging remission.

God's free choice

A first reaction is sympathy with Cain. No reason is even suggested why his sacrifice is rejected and his brother's accepted. Humanly speaking, he had every right to be exasperated and jealous. But time and again in the scriptures God chooses the young brother, Jacob over his brother Esau, Joseph in preference to all his elder brothers.

The first king, Saul, was chosen from the smallest clan of the smallest tribe. The forgotten youngest, David, was anointed by Samuel in preference to his fine, upstanding brothers. God's choice is free and cannot be earned. Like the potter, says the prophet Jeremiah, he makes one vessel so and another so. 'Can a pot say of the potter, "He does not know his job?"' (Isaiah 29:16). Like the labourers in Jesus' parable, paid at random for their work in the vineyard, human beings cannot enter into reckoning with God.

There may be details of my character, personality, physique, fortune that I would rather be without, but I suspect that most of us have enough self-love to prefer being ourselves to someone else. And a comforting thought is that God, too, loves me just as I am. He even lovingly put a mark on Cain to protect him from vengeance.

PRAYER

Lord, you accept me as I am. Remove from me all petty jealousy of the talents, opportunities and success of others. Keep me content to praise you for what I am and for what you have given me.

5

Patriarchs before the Flood

The blessing of life

The Bible now gives us a list of ten successive generations from Adam to Noah. They all lived to an immense age, the eldest of course being Methuselah, who lived 969 years. There is, of course, no significance in the upside-down numerals of this age, for the Hebrews used letters for numbers. Indeed the exact ages given to these early fathers of the people differ in the different traditions of the text of the Bible. The point is the extraordinary length of their ages, for long life was considered the sign of God's favour and blessing on these revered, early members of the family of God.

Such is our fear of dying (not, I think, so much of being dead) that even Christians today unreflectively consider long life to be a blessing, something to thank God for, when really the Christian should be looking forward avidly to the fullness of company with God in eternal life. But the earliest members at the beginning of the Judeo-Christian tradition had as yet no such concepts.

In this, as in so many other ways, the revelation of God's love was a gradual process. Christians perceive that full enjoyment of the presence of God is the only tolerable conclusion of God's overflowing love, but it was only gradually that this became clear.

In the earliest parts of the Bible, the basic unit was not so much the individual as the nomadic clan, wandering from place to place with their flocks and tents, returning annually to a sort of tribal centre where their dead were buried. The fortunes of the whole tribe were very much joined together. Consequently the idea of death was 'being joined to the forefathers': the dead person simply slipped back and was absorbed into the tribal stem. This attitude goes from Abraham at least to David, who mourned his baby son: 'I shall go to him, but he cannot come back to me' (2 Samuel 12:23).

This idea gave way to a view of Sheol, a dark and dusty place where the dead live a sort of unsatisfying, shadowy half-life, devoid of vigour and power, and unable to praise God. There the dead sink into oblivion. The most the kings of the earth there can do when the king of Babylon arrives is to greet him, 'So, you too are now as weak as we are, under you a mattress of maggots, over you a blanket of worms' (Isaiah 14:10–11). It is like life in a dusty, endless waiting-room, from which there is no release.

The spirited Job has no qualms about questioning accepted views, and refuses to be satisfied. He demands something more positive. Though he cannot yet see how this can be, he will not accept that Sheol is final: 'Will no one hide me in Sheol, and shelter me there till your anger is past? Day after day of my service, I should be waiting for my relief to come' (Job 14:13–14).

In a great cry of despairing confidence he insists, 'I know that I have a living Defender! After my awakening he will set me close to him, and from my flesh I shall look on God. My eyes will be gazing on no stranger' (19:25–26). The love of God cannot relinquish what it has once grasped. This was why Jesus taught of the God of Abraham, the God of Isaac and the God of Jacob, 'God is a God of the living, not of the dead' (Mark 12:27), why Paul longs to be dissolved and to be with Christ, and why John speaks of eternal life.

Enoch

By contrast to the other long-lived early fathers, Enoch lived a mere 365 years—and this time there must be a significance in the number of years for it totals the number of days in the year. Then he 'was no more, because God took him'. The Bible does not elaborate on this, but Jewish tradition regarded it as a mark of special love and favour.

PRAYER

Lord, let me see long life as a blessing because it is a prolonged preparation for union with you. May I be ready for you whenever you wish to take me.

6 The crime of the sons of God

The context of this strange little episode suggests that it is seen as one more example of the spread of the corruption which will lead to the cleansing of the world by the Flood. In some non-biblical Jewish traditions it has been regarded as the story of the origin of evil, rivalling or even taking the place of the story of the Fall of Adam and Eve.

In this case, we now have examples of a third kind of transgression, a sexual mismatch, after the pride and independence of Eve, and the jealousy of Cain. Judaism had a horror of mixtures, the yoking of two different kinds of animals together, the combination of different kinds of cloth. This may stem from anxiety to avoid Canaanite magical practices which made plentiful use of odd combinations. In this context a sexual mismatch would be all the more horrific.

The origin of giants

The biblical author who arranged these chapters seems to have taken an ancient story which explained the origin of superhuman beings in the legendary past as a mixture of human and divine. They are here called 'nephilim', giants or heroes. The sons of God who fathered them may well have been in the original, pre-Hebrew story divine beings, gods of the Canaanite pantheon.

In later tradition the expression 'sons of God' is frequently used for angels, and this may have given rise to the whole idea of the sinful union of fallen angels with women. In later centuries of Judaism, approaching the time of Jesus, speculations about good and evil spirits became so important that this story was easily pressed into service to explain the fall of some of the angels as due to their lust for women.

God's decision as a result comes in two parts. First God decides to limit human life to the span which we know; no longer will human beings be blessed with the length of life which the first ten generations enjoyed. Then evil reaches such a pitch that God decides that both humans and animals must be totally destroyed, and the scene is set for the Flood.

The fallen angels

Fallen angels, led by Lucifer, the prince of evil spirits, feature quite largely and luridly in medieval imagery. In the Bible they appear only in two sparse mentions among various examples of due punishment for sin: God did not spare the fallen angels (2 Peter 2:4 and Jude 6). Their importance in popular imagination comes from Jewish legend rather than from any Christian source. This in turn is influenced by the Persian doctrines of spirits in the final centuries before Christ.

The important message of this passage is that evil is simply incompatible with the nature of God. In many cultures even the gods themselves can sin. In Greek culture perhaps the supreme example is the scene of the gods convulsed by uncontrollable laughter at finding the divine spouse of Zeus in the act of adultery. In Mesopotamian myths it was the childish squabbling of the gods which led eventually to the creation of the world. The Hebrew concept of God is too serious to admit of any such trifling with morality. Human standards can only hope to follow in the image of God, never to surpass it.

PRAYER

God, create in me a pure heart,
renew within me a resolute spirit,
do not thrust me away from your presence,
do not take away from me your spirit of holiness.
Psalm 51

7

The Flood

Two accounts joined together

At first sight the story of the Flood appears to be repetitive. There are two decisions to destroy the world, two entries into the ark; the flood comes twice and ends twice, etc. In fact this is because there are two different versions of the story joined together.

This is only one instance, perhaps the most obvious, of something which happens often in the early traditions of the Bible. There were two, often three, versions, probably oral, of the same story handed down independently. These streams of tradition each have their recognizable characteristics.

We have already, for instance, come across one particular set of interests in the first creation story and in the list of early fathers, the ten generations from Adam. This is one stream of tradition, known as the Priestly writer (or P) because its interests centre on matters of concern to the Israelite priesthood in Babylon, the sabbath, matters of purity, clean and unclean food, genealogies.

In the Flood story this is the leading narrative. It can be recognized in the careful listing of Noah's family, its distinction between clean and unclean animals, the dating in Noah's 600th year, the repeated 150 days.

Into this story is worked another, named after the name it uses for God, the Yahwist: it uses the name 'Yahweh' (often translated 'the LORD') although this name was not revealed until the time of Moses. In general it shows more concern with story-telling and warm characterization; especially God is warm, kindly and thoughtful. This stream of tradition has been seen in the stories of Adam and Eve and of Cain and Abel. In the Flood narrative it is marked by the name 'Yahweh', by the repeated number forty and by less exact time-indications.

The Flood in other literature

A story of a disastrous flood occurs in many other literatures. In some African literatures this is a punishment for human sin. But the closest version, which is obviously related to the biblical story, is in the Mesopotamian *Epic of Gilgamesh*, which exists in several versions. Here there is the same command from the god to Gilgamesh to build a huge boat by which some humans and animals may be saved, the same sending out of a dove to see eventually that the flood has subsided, and the same sacrifice to the gods at the end. But in the Babylonian story there is no moral dimension involved. The disaster is not a punishment for sin, but simply the result of childish petulance by the gods.

The message of the story

Here again, as in the story of the Fall, we have an instance of the Hebrew story adopting the common stock of Babylonian myth and adapting it to express their own morality and God-centred view of the world. In the flat plains of Mesopotamia a slight rise in the level of the great rivers Tigris and Euphrates would flood a large area. The common basis may well be a memory of some such flood. To a local community such a flood could 'destroy all living things under heaven having the breath of life' (Genesis 6:17).

The remote memory of such an archetypical disaster is used in the story of Noah's flood to underline in an unforgettable way a religious message. The awesome power of God has total control of the whole world. The values of a whole civilization may become so corrupt that it becomes odious and intolerable to the sanctity of God. Nevertheless, the individual may stand against them, and may indeed win for those under the protection of such a group exemption from divine rejection.

Without waiting for another such flood disaster, any civilization with a universally accepted system of values needs to question whether divine values and aims have become so neglected that the conventional values need to be swept totally away.

PRAYER

Lord God, ruler of the universe, grant me to remain ever alert to your values and critical of generally accepted morality. Help me to examine myself and to strive to maintain what you show me to be right.

8 The new world order

An enduring world order

After the world has been cleansed by the Flood, it gets a new start, with a guarantee that such a radical break will never recur. A promise is given, first 'as long as earth endures' (8:22), then 'for all ages to come' (9:12). Does this promise mean that the world is set for all eternity?

What, then, of the later teaching in the Prophets on the Day of the Lord, or the teaching in the Gospels on the final judgment at the end of the world, or Paul's expectancy that Christ will hand the kingdom back to his Father, 'when he has put all things under his feet'? What of the Second Law of Thermodynamics and the confident expectation that our solar system will, after a due number of millions of years, collapse? To treat the Bible as a scientific textbook is a hopeless mis-understanding. The word of God is intended to reveal to us the nature of God's love for us, to enable us to have some glimpse of the divine nature, and to teach us the way to God. Any other treatment of the Bible is at best working across the grain, at worst mere superstition and magic.

A covenant with Noah

A covenant offered by God to his chosen ones will be an important fea-ture of the developing relationship between God and his people. This covenant with Noah is the first; the renewal of the relationship is described in terms of the later covenant relationship with Abraham and with Moses. The classic covenant is a two-sided relationship, a promise of protection on certain terms. Thus the covenant with Moses demands that Israel obey the terms of loyalty detailed in the Law.

This covenant, however, is different: there are no terms that Noah must obey; it is a pure act of grace, friendship and love, offered unconditionally. Nor is this covenant restricted to any particular group of people: it is a covenant with the world order itself, 'you and your descendants', but also 'every living creature'.

The guarantee of the covenant is the rainbow, a symbol which continues to thrill the human heart. Legends about the rainbow show the echo which this mysterious, evanescent light effect evokes. The pot of gold at the end of the rainbow is only a more materialistic version of the hope it engenders. 'Where the rainbow ends...' is the stuff of countless songs. Appearing as the sun shines after rain, it is the symbol of freshness, renewal, positive hope, fertility.

The rainbow really is a natural expression of blessing on the world. Our enduring childhood's wonder at it is the stuff of prayer.

The Priestly source

The interests of the Priestly source are clear in several ways in this passage: the immediate recourse to a thanksgiving-sacrifice according to the later conventions of sacrifice, the distinction between clean and unclean foods, the prohibition of eating blood. This version of the tradition is always concerned to show that the institutions of Israelite religion are part of the fabric of existence, having existed for countless ages.

The prohibition of blood is a valuable symbol. It may spring from primitive science and primitive tabu, but its natural imagery is powerful. No one who has seen the slaughter of an animal, particularly a large and powerful animal like a bull, can be blind to the emotional link between blood and life.

Blood flows in streams as life departs, leaving what was a noble and powerful beast as no more than a hunk of meat. The pathetic trail of blood, left as a wounded wild animal creeps off to its dying shelter, leaves no doubt that as blood seeps away, so does life itself. So to claim the blood for God alone is a brilliant statement of God's ownership of life, his gift of life to all that lives, and his continuing care of that life, so long as the blood remains, pumping from the heart.

Not perhaps wholly logical, there is yet something attractive and honourable about the vegetarian's added distaste for red meat. A symbolic protest, no doubt, but a recognition of the sanctity of life and our duty to care for the world around us.

PRAYER

Lord, by your covenant with Noah you renewed your blessing on your creation. Grant me renewed awareness of your presence in your creation. Grant me to value and enjoy these signs of your blessing, and lead me always to praise you.

9 The descendants of Noah

The table of peoples

The chief part of this section is another list of generations or descendants, similar to chapter 5. The Priestly tradition gives us these lists from time to time. It is obviously more than a simple list of descendants, but serves as a geographical and ethnic division. Enough of the names are known to make it clear that the names are not those of individuals but of towns and regions, perhaps on the assumption that one ancestor who gave his name to a town was responsible for the peopling of it.

Japheth's sons include the territory to the north and west of Palestine. Javan is the name normally used for Greece, and the Kittim for the Greek islands.

Ham's sons take the south. Mizraim remains the name for Egypt. Cush recurs as Ethiopia, or even black Africa in general. Sheba will provide the famous queen who came from the south to see Solomon. It is a little surprising that Canaan is included; it is more or less coterminous with the present Palestine, and is used for the civilization which preceded the Israelite invasion under Joshua.

This may be the link, for in the centuries before the settlement of Israel there, the land was closely controlled by Egypt. The great Egyptian fortresses are still to be seen, such as Megiddo, Taanach, Beth Shean; Megiddo was strategically important even in the First World War. Canaan's own sons include towns on the borders of this area, like Sodom and Sidon, but also the peoples of the ancient cities of the land, such as Jebusites, who held Jerusalem till it was captured by David.

To the east come the sons of Shem, or (roughly) Semites. They include the resounding names of the great civilizations of Mesopotamia, such as Elam and Asshur, whose libraries have been discovered in recent centuries, with inestimable contributions to our understanding of the Bible. Among them too are the mysterious lands of the east, like Uz, the land of wise men and wizards.

The list proclaims the unity of the inhabitants of the known world, for all are descended from Noah; even these remote and powerful lands have no independent origin. More importantly it also claims them all for God. So soon after the blessing covenanted to Noah, all the nations can be seen to enjoy the benefits of those blessings. It is a positive and optimistic statement.

Noah's drunkenness

The unsavoury little incident inserted just after the introduction of Noah's three sons completes the circle of disorder in this first glimpse of the world. In the story of Adam and Eve we had the husband–wife relationship; in Cain and Abel the strife between brother and brother; now we have disrespect (as well as reverence) between children and parent.

The advance from simple agriculture to vine-growing brings its own dangers. Like any advance in civilization, it is liable to abuse. Nowhere, however, does the Bible suggest that the abuse of wine should lead to its total ban. On the contrary, wine is often favourably mentioned in the Bible among the gifts of God's blessing.

There is no need to suppose that Ham committed incest with his father, though the expression 'to see the nakedness' of someone can carry that sense. The sin of disrespect to the very fatherhood of his father is quite sufficient. It was unfortunate enough to stumble carelessly on this shame of his father, but instead of remedying the situation, Ham merely chatters about it to his brothers.

PRAYER

Lord, the nations are becoming more and more aware in our day of their interdependence and need for each other. Make us aware of the sin of racial disharmony and help us to remove it. Help us truly to appreciate both the differences between us and what we share with each other.

10 The tower of Babel

The final story of the primitive history of humanity seems in some ways to double as another story of the origins of evil. Again the fault is pride and attempting to do by personal efforts what should have been left to God. Alternatively it may be regarded as a different account of the diversification of the peoples, corresponding to the list of chapter 10, but concentrating on how they split up, rather than on the end result.

This would be an excellent example of the different approaches of the Priestly and the Yahwistic traditions: the former gives a detailed or even exhaustive list; the latter offers a lively, suggestive narrative, with plenty of character but not much detail of the peoples.

It is amusing that the writer needs to explain the building-materials: his audience is clearly unfamiliar with the Babylonian materials, bricks and bitumen, explaining them as the equivalent to the stone and mortar commonly used in the rocky Israelite hill-country. The point of the story is already suggested by the seemingly unmotivated fear of the tower-builders that they may get scattered all over the world.

The whole is nicely topped off by the pun, 'Babel', the name of the town, being associated with the very 'balel', which means 'confuse, confound'. Such puns on names are much beloved of biblical authors. With this the English word 'babble' is associated, though in fact it derives from the inarticulate sounds of baby talk.

The tower-builders wish to reach up to heaven by their own initiative; do they wish to become gods, or to have direct communication with the deity, or simply to build an outstandingly tall tower? It is certainly some manifestation of pride.

Isaiah's satire on the fallen king of Babylon describes the same phenomenon, 'How did you come to be thrown to the ground, conqueror of nations? You who used to think to yourself, I shall scale the heavens; higher than the stars of God I shall set my throne' (Isaiah 14:12–13). Similarly Ezekiel's satire on the fall of Tyre mocks the city, 'Because your heart has grown proud you thought, I am a god. I am divinely enthroned far out to sea' (Ezekiel 28:2). To build a high tower was to make a proud claim to divine power.

Ziggurats

This complex of ideas, of idolatrous claims to divine power, was no doubt related to the ziggurats of Mesopotamia. These were towering temples, built solid in receding steps, and reaching up some sixty to seventy metres. The act of worship took place on the top.

Over two centuries ago the ziggurat of Borsippa, a few kilometres south of Babylon, was hailed as the original tower of Babel. It still stands thirty-five metres high, and shows clear traces on the top of a vertical cleft and mud-bricks vitrified by the heat of a lightning-strike. In the excitement of the discovery, this evidence of a lightning-strike was taken as the manifestation of God's vengeance.

Pentecost

In the Christian tradition the miracle of languages at Pentecost is understood as the reversal of the scattering of the peoples at Babel. The ability of the people of so many nations all to understand the same language is a sign of the beginning of the restored unity of the world. It overcomes the disunity and hostility of the scattered nations, making them again into one united community. It therefore presages the coming of peace and harmony which is to be brought into being by the outpouring of the Spirit.

PRAYER

Lord, by this second appearance of pride you warn us against the arrogance of human achievements. If we build our towers and empires, help us to ensure that we remain within the limits you set, and give the praise to you.

11
GENESIS 12:1-9
The call of Abraham

Abraham's call is the most significant moment in the history of Israel—or to the Christian believer in all history, apart from the events of Jesus' death and resurrection. This is where the story begins: we are all children of Abraham. At this moment begins the continuous history of the Hebrew people, though not yet in the form of modern history such as we would expect to find in a modern textbook.

Ur of the Chaldees

The civilization from which Abraham was drawn was a magnificent one. The great ziggurat of Ur of the Chaldees on the Mesopotamian plain near the Persian Gulf still towers 200 feet above the plain. In the royal tombs discovered by Sir Leonard Woolley in 1925, the gold wreaths and statuettes and finely carved jade figurines vie with the tomb of Tutankhamun. Like many peoples on this open, burningly hot plain, they worshipped the sun and the moon, which frequently occur in their jewelry.

All this was Abraham summoned to leave. He was called to give up the sophistication and splendour of this merchant city for a dirty, solitary nomad's goat-hair tent, surrounded by sand, ashes of burnt-out cooking-fires and animal droppings.

An unknown God

By whom? By an unknown God, who simply promised to be Abraham's personal protector. Why should Abraham believe that his name was to be famous, that all nations would bless themselves by him? He knew nothing of what we know about God, not even his name. He was known simply as 'the god of Abraham'. Later the same God received two more equally awesome and impersonal titles, 'the Fear of Isaac' and 'the Mighty One of Jacob', as this personal bond was confirmed respectively to Isaac and Jacob.

The full realization that God was the creator and master of the universe did not become clear to Israel for another thousand years, at the time of the Babylonian exile. No idea of the unfailing love of God, as revealed to the prophet Hosea. No Law, no sacrifice, no sabbath. Did Israel's loyalty to God even exclude reverence to other deities? The only firm bond was the certainty that in the hands of this protector Abraham's person and family were safe. How? No details.

The starkness of the desert

There is a certain starkness about this engagement, like the starkness of the desert itself. In the desert there is no concealment and no pretence. All is exposed on the flat sand, under the burning sun. No corners on the road, no bushes or rocks for shade, no shoots of vegetation to nourish hope. Only pitiless confrontation with the absolute.

There is a quiet ferocity about the desert which drives the human mind to God in helpless weakness. Like other desert religions, Abraham's relationship to God brooked no images. No picturing or imagining can suffice to portray the awesome God who fills the horizon. It is not surprising that both Judaism and Islam refuse to have any representation of God. This would be a limiting and trivializing factor, cutting down an awesome divinity to something which the human imagination can cope with. Islam does have the sacred black stone at Mecca, but its very facelessness is itself significant.

For Paul, Abraham is the model of faith, I think, for two reasons. Firstly, because of the contrast between what he had and the way of life he accepted, a way of life which is intrinsically unstable and haphazard, deprived of all security in itself. Secondly, because of the unreasoning faith he showed. He asked for no proof and received none; he simply relied on the word of promise and so on the personality behind it.

PRAYER

God of Abraham, we still know you so little, but you call us to put all our trust in you. When all around is desert, grant me confidence in your loving care.

GENESIS 12:10–20

12 Abram in Egypt

The oral tradition

We now embark upon the stories of the patriarchs, the original fathers of the people of Israel. These are tales passed down by word of mouth round campfires, at water holes, at family gatherings and at markets—wherever members of the tribes met together and passed on the traditions of their people. The nature of the story-telling corresponds to this sort of occasion rather than to the conventions of modern academic historians or law courts. They are no less true for that. Had they been otherwise, it is unlikely that they would have survived!

It is a good deal easier to remember and repeat a well-told story than to pass on a dry, analytical account. But we should expect a certain concentration on the essential point of a story at the expense of some of the details. In telling a good story the exaggeration or simplification of details is perfectly legitimate. Indeed, a good story-teller rejoices to weave a story slightly differently at each telling.

Nevertheless, in these stories of the patriarchs unimportant details are often preserved with almost unbelievable fidelity. Recent archaeological finds have given us considerable knowledge of the laws and customs of the times. Again and again these are reflected in the stories, although such details often had no sense or significance when the stories were still being told, nearly a thousand years after the original happenings.

The faithful repetition of stories for so many centuries is in itself an extraordinary testimony to the value the Hebrews put on their tradition. They knew that they were the heirs of the promises made by God to their forefathers. Every detail of the way God had cherished and favoured them remained important to them—as it is also to us.

Sarai saved from Pharaoh

Hardly had the promise been given, when disaster nearly struck: had Sarai been carried off into the Pharaoh's harem, that would have been the end of the story. It was the divine warning that prevented it, for God had yet to fulfil his promise and could not let it falter so soon. Credit can hardly go to Abram.

There is surely some humour in showing the cowardliness of the great father of the people of promise! He is perfectly willing to sacrifice his wife, and is concerned only to save his own skin and even make a little profit. Beyond the humour there is also the more serious lesson that God's promises do not depend on human strength or resolution. However weak his human instruments, God still wins through!

The subterfuge of Abram is explained by a horror of adultery: it was perfectly acceptable for the Egyptian to take an unmarried girl into his harem, but not to commit adultery against another man. Hence Abram's pretence that the woman he has with him is his sister rather than his wife.

In fact she may have been both wife and sister, at any rate legally. Recent discoveries have shown that in calling her his sister he may not have been lying, though certainly suppressing the more important truth. Ancient legislation allowed a man to enhance his wife's status by adopting her also as his sister: Abram makes use of this custom to divert attention from her marital situation.

To those with experience of modern Bedouin encampments it may seem unlikely that the great Pharaoh, ruler of Upper and Lower Egypt, with his sophisticated and luxurious court, should have fallen for a nomad's wife. This is precisely where the canons of story-telling and academic history differ: in the conventions of the former it is a pardonable exaggeration that a village headman should be described as Pharaoh.

PRAYER

Father, you protect us from ourselves. However weak we are, you still accomplish your purpose through us. Grant me to bask in your strength, and also to join with you steadfastly in your purposes.

13 Abram and Lot separate

Abram the nomad

The picture of Abram given us by the Bible is that of a petty nomad. He roams the countryside with flocks of sheep and goats, carrying all his goods on a couple of donkeys. Even nowadays these would consist virtually only of a large goat-hair tent, a mattress or two, a few rugs and cooking-pots (sometimes a battered transistor radio). He can move away, leaving the tent open and untenanted, because there is nothing to steal. He avoids the centres of population, but often stays near them because they have the water and the fertile ground.

Abram is *between* Bethel and Ai, and settles at the Oak of Mamre *near* Hebron. Water can be fetched in sheepskin gourds or pottery pitchers from the town's source of water, and there will be grazing for the flocks on the margins of the settled area. It is a way of life that makes a modern gypsy caravan look gold-plated. All the nomad's wealth is in his family and his flocks.

After his pay-off in Egypt, Abram's wealth has increased. We need not imagine his sheep and goats noisily thronging the countryside, for the grazing area required per beast on the margins of the desert would be 20–30 times that required on a home-farm.

Even today, when income can be supplemented by selling simple herbs in the towns, it is rare to see more than two or three tents together; the land simply cannot provide support. If the flock begins to grow, movement of flocks to find grazing soon becomes wide-ranging; disputes between herdsmen over the better grazing areas will soon flare.

Separation

The story of Lot presupposes that the Dead Sea area, under which Sodom and Gomorrah are assumed to be submerged, is still fertile country. The phenomenon of the Dead Sea, evil-smelling, surrounded by hostile rocks, devoid of fish, vegetation, birds (the Greeks called it 'the Birdless Sea') has at least not yet infected that area. The area still enjoys the more savoury name of 'the Jordan plain'. It is certainly true that the irrigated areas to the north and south-east of the Dead Sea are lusciously fertile. Given water, the warmth at this lowest spot on the earth's surface produces fast-growing crops in abundance.

So Lot chooses for himself this attractive countryside, now vanished but imagined to be like 'the garden of the Lord' or the Delta of Egypt. In so doing he deserts the Promised Land—with the consequences which will soon become clear.

Abram had given Lot the choice, with extraordinary generosity, all the more generous in a patriarchal situation where Abram was very definitely the head of the clan. It is anyway a sad decision for Abram: he still has no heir, and now loses a possible substitute and family help. Lot's choice means also that he loses the more fertile territory.

It all means that Abram is cast back even more strictly onto the promise of the God who appeared to him. No distraction or let-out is allowed. To emphasize the point, the promise is now repeated.

PRAYER

Lord, your servant Abraham put nothing before your promise, and placed all his trust in that alone. Enable me to make your promise of life and of intimacy with you the sole motivation in my life too.

14 GENESIS 14
The campaign of the four great kings

The story of this campaign has puzzled historians. From a literary point of view the story is quite unlike any of the other narratives of Abram. The four great kings are not the petty chieftains with whom Abram is used to dealing, but are rulers of great empires.

The names of the kings do not fit any period of history, nor is co-operation between these empires likely, still less against little town-ships in the Jordan Valley. The suggestion that Abram defeated them in battle is absurd, though the Bible only actually says that he recovered the spoil, without detailing how this happened. Another difficulty is that 'Hobah, north of Damascus' is hundreds of miles outside Abram's range.

There are odd little features of the narrative which might provide clues. What function have the 'bitumen wells in the Valley of Siddim'? This might be a clue that this story basically explains features of the landscape, like the explanation of the Cave of Makkedah in Joshua 10:27. What is the purpose or symbolism of the number of retainers, 318, whom Abram took with him? Since numbers are represented by letters of the alphabet, there may be some hidden meaning here.

In view of these bristling difficulties, it may be best to conclude that we cannot now recover the episode on which this story is built. The writer is using names drawn from world history, the names of these great empires, to show that Abram enjoyed special divine protection, which extended even to military prowess.

It is a story which would have touched a chord in an audience familiar with these great empires of the East. It is also a merited humiliation for Lot, after his desertion of the land of promise in favour of the luxuriant Jordan Valley, and a further instance of Abram's generous loyalty towards him.

Melchizedek

The mysterious incident of Melchizedek has inspired Christian tradition from the Letter to the Hebrews onwards. Historically, this 'king of Salem' is no doubt king of Jerusalem. His name means 'my king is justice', and is closely related to the name of David's priest, Zadok. Presumably David, in capturing Jerusalem, took over the priesthood of that city also, who saw its ancestry in Melchizedek.

The contact here between Abram and Melchizedek is therefore all the more significant as the first contact between the Hebrew nomad and the city of Jerusalem. There is a courteous exchange between them, the priest-king giving his blessing, and Abram replying with material gifts.

A further dimension is added to the Melchizedek tradition by Psalm 110, which pronounces the Messiah to be 'a priest for ever, of the order of Melchizedek'. This means that the expected figure is to be heir to the priestly traditions of Jerusalem as well as to the royal traditions of David. The psalm has been important in Christian tradition, quoted by Paul and in the Gospels on the lips of Jesus, of the exaltation of Jesus in power at the right hand of the Father.

The Letter to the Hebrews uses the psalm to depict Christ's priesthood as following that of Melchizedek. Christ's priesthood, which is not and cannot be of the Levitical order, is of a new order, which is at the same time a return to the older order of Melchizedek. The mysterious and unannounced appearance of Melchizedek is seen as an image of the eternity of Christ's priesthood, having neither beginning or end.

Thus for the Christian Melchizedek represents a wonderful unity of biblical tradition, integrating the beginnings of revelation at the time of Abraham with its fulfilment in Christ. The campaign of the four kings is mysterious. Melchizedek himself is mysterious. Yet the whole incident serves to suggest the forward thrust of God's plan, already aimed towards Christ.

PRAYER

Father, in your priest-king Melchizedek you somehow prefigured Christ your son. We thank you for your continuous care of your people from that day to this, and your gradual revelation of your love and wisdom.

15 The covenant with Abram

The covenant with Noah had consisted in an open covenant for the whole human race, but now God makes a special covenant with Abram, making Abram and his family specially chosen. In one sense this is only a repetition of the call in chapter 12; in another it is an important new stage in which God formally binds himself by ritual. In this sense it already looks forward to the definitive covenant on Sinai which embraces the whole people of Israel.

The incident begins with an assurance by God, which is little more than a repetition of the promise given in chapter 12. But this time Abram demurs and questions God's earnestness, since he is childless.

The horror of childlessness appears on two levels: firstly, the primitive state of belief in a future after death makes continuance of the line by means of children all the more important; the dead person simply returns to the fathers, and an heir carries on his personality.

Secondly, in a primitive desert nomadic existence, old people, unsupported by the vigour of youth, are in a truly sorry state. It is common enough today in Palestine that when a father has a son he deserts his own name and renames himself the father of his son: Abu Dahud, the father of David. So important is an heir. If Abram has no heir of his family, he will have to adopt a member of his household as his heir, a process well-attested in ancient Mesopotamian legislation.

The faith of Abram

After the repetition of the promise, however, comes the first crucial reference to Abram's faith, which 'was reckoned to him as uprightness' (NRSV and many modern translations use the word 'righteousness'). For Christians this statement is irrevocably marked by the use made of it by Paul in his Letters to the Galatians and Romans. There he uses it in a particular theological context, controversy over the value and function of the Mosaic Law. Paul insists that no observance of the Law can merit uprightness: God's original promise, long before the Law was given, was not to those who observed the Law, but to those who had faith in him, a faith which is now fulfilled in Christ, his Son.

The sense of two words, 'faith' and 'uprightness', to the Hebrew mind is clearly crucial. The latter concept is straightforward enough: there is no lack or deficiency in something 'upright'. An upright weight is the true, correct weight, not one which defrauds. Someone who rightly wins, in a battle or controversy as well as a law court, is vindicated and is considered upright. People who are true to themselves and their promises are upright. It is perhaps, as much as anything, a conception of wholeness. So for Abram this made him all he should be, this was all that was necessary, he was complete and pleasing to God.

The idea behind 'faith' here is nothing to do with intellectual belief. The basic idea here expressed by 'put his faith' is finding reliability, firmness and stability. The root word is 'Amen'. 'Amen' is a response and an acceptance. You say a prayer and I add 'Amen' to express that it is my prayer too. You challenge me to an oath and I say 'Amen' to show that I bind myself by that oath. I make that prayer or that oath firm. So when Paul calls Christ the 'Amen' of the Father (2 Corinthians 1:19–20), he means that in Christ the promises of the Father are realized and fulfilled. So in this case of Abram it means he placed all his confidence in God and ceased to worry.

The ritual

The scene of the covenant is mysterious and awesome, in the darkness after sunset, when a trance or a deep, dark dread has come upon Abram. Is it a dream or a waking reality? The ritual of cleaving the victims in two has a magical origin: may the two halves come together again if I break my oath. Normally the two parties making the pact or contract take the path between the halves of the victims. In this case only God, under the awesome image of the smoking torch, takes the path, for the pact is one-sided: God is binding himself, and Abram is only the recipient of the promise.

PRAYER

Lord God, Abram found his stability in you, and that was all he needed. Whatever turmoil, worries and upsets come my way, grant me this trust of Abram, and the confidence that you will support me and bring me through them.

16 The birth of Ishmael

The legal background

To understand this somewhat strange story it is important to know some of the background of contemporary Near Eastern law. We have already considered the importance of an heir, especially for desert nomads. If a wife was barren, she could present to her husband one of her slave-girls, considered as a sort of seedbed, who would then provide her husband with an heir in her place. In some legislation the true, barren, wife then has authority over her slave-girl's child.

There were obvious dangers in this process, among them the danger of the slave-girl supplanting her mistress in her husband's affection, the mistress becoming jealous, insults and rivalry in either direction. The legal system, which was far from primitive, laid down in detail the rights and obligations of the three parties involved, and also of the children. In the worst instance, if the slave-girl taunted her mistress, the mistress could demand that she be expelled. Sarai seems to have taken a slightly different course of action, which led to the same result! But the Bible is not concerned to accuse or justify the actors involved in this drama, and does not explain to us where the blame lay.

The Angel of the Lord

This is the first of many appearances of the Angel of the Lord. This Angel is not like other angels, but is a special figure, appearing with special frequency in these early stories of the patriarchs, and only rarely later. 'Angel', of course, means 'messenger'. In many ways the Angel of the Lord seems to be equated with God himself.

The Angel of the Lord is a vehicle for solving the problem of maintaining two important theological positions, God's awesome and unapproachable transcendence, and God's intimate and loving concern with human affairs. So here the Angel of the Lord speaks to Hagar, and she considers that the Lord himself has spoken to her.

Similarly, in the story of Jacob, the Angel of the Lord claims the title of 'the God who appeared to you at Bethel' (Genesis 32:13). The Angel of the Lord is a sort of visible manifestation of God, a way in which God may be seen at work in the world without actually making God visible and audible.

The ethnic dimension

In these early stories there is often a shimmering between individuals and the tribe they represent, and they reflect each other. So in this case the tribe of the Ishmaelites are seen in their ancestor Ishmael, and their qualities are attributed to him. They receive the same blessing of becoming numerous as Abram himself had received. To the later descendants of Isaac and Jacob, beginning to become sedentary and agricultural, the wild and lawless raiders from the desert were a threat. They could sweep out of the desert in the south and vanish back to it with their booty.

This is why Ishmael is given the destiny of being 'a wild donkey of a man, his hand against every man, and every man's hand against him'. Part of David's success, as he rose to power in the southern tribe of Judah, was that he managed to police and control these wild raiders.

The well of Lahai Roi was probably the tribal centre of the Ishmaelites, deep in the Negeb. Its name is given a meaning by this story, in a typical Hebrew way. All names were felt to be significant, and were attached, often with considerable strain, to meaningful words with a similar sound. The name *El Roi* of itself means the God of Roi, so the God who is worshipped at or by Roi. The meaning which Hagar gives to 'Roi' is strained and depends on popular etymology and what it meant at the time.

The story shows the difficult relationship between these two related peoples. It attributes this, too, to God who blesses each nation and tribe in the way he wills.

PRAYER

Lord God, you are the Father of all humanity, even of those tribes or nations which disagree with us or oppose our interests. Grant me tolerance towards others, and an ability to see their point of view.

17 Covenant and circumcision

A covenant with obligations

We have already read about Abram's call with a promise from the Lord, and about the mysterious covenant cut (in Hebrew you '*cut* a covenant') by means of the passage between the halves of the victims. That was a one-sided covenant, by which the Lord imposed obligations on himself without seemingly demanding corresponding duties from Abram.

Now comes a different account, stemming from the Priestly tradition. This imposes obligations on Abram and, as a sign of a new relationship, a new name on both him and his wife. The obligations are moral, religious and ritual: moral, the daunting challenge to be perfect; religious, to have God as their God for ever; and ritual, to be circumcised.

The repeated reference to fatherhood of many nations, and to the covenant made with him, serve to stress the central point of his importance: he is the first link in the chain of the promise which Israel inherited, and on which Israel's existence depended. In Islam he is called 'the friend of God'.

Circumcision

The exact significance of the removal of the foreskin of the male member is not clear. In origin it may be a measure of hygiene. In most nations where it was practised in the ancient world it was connected with puberty, preparation for sexual intercourse and for full adult membership of the tribe. Egyptian texts suggest that it included a test of bravery in accepting the pain without crying out. As a religious rite it no doubt included the idea of consecrating to God the means of generation, a recognition that life and its reproduction belong to God alone.

For Israel, however, it became the principal sign of membership of the covenant people, performed eight days after the birth of a male child. It is not clear how unique Israel was among its neighbours in practising circumcision in ancient times. Certainly circumcision, like other ritual distinguishing practices (sabbath and food laws) began to gain its full importance only during the Babylonian exile, when the Israelites needed to assert their difference from those around them. In the early legal texts it is mentioned only twice, which suggests that it was not seen to have major significance.

At the same time as stressing the importance of this physical operation, the prophetic texts of the period of the Exile stress the importance of 'circumcision of the heart'. Circumcision itself has no value unless it is a sign of wholehearted devotion and commitment to God's covenant.

Names

Throughout biblical history naming was a sign of taking possession and control. By naming the beasts Adam asserted his mastery over them. Jesus imposes a new name and a new function on Simon, calling him Peter and making him the Rock of his new Israel. These names normally have a significance, or, if they do not, are given one! This may involve a rather strained pun, as the well of Lahai Roi in the previous chapter. 'Abram' and 'Abraham' are in fact alternative forms of the same name, meaning 'great through his father', and the meaning 'father of a multitude' would fit the name 'Abhamon'.

In the same way, 'Sarah' and 'Sarai' are alternative forms of the same name, meaning 'princess'. The surprising mention of Abraham's laughter is the first of several allusions to the name 'Isaac'. At various times Sarah, Abraham and Isaac himself are said to smile or laugh—in justification of the name. *Yitzhaq*, which becomes 'Isaac' via Greek and Latin transliterations, means 'he will laugh/smile', though the original form was probably *yitzhaq-el*, 'God will smile on him'.

PRAYER

Father, you gave your people circumcision as an external sign of their devotion to your covenant. Grant that in me and in your Church external signs may not slide into hypocrisy, but may always be signs of our real devotion to you.

18 The Angel of the Lord visits Abraham

Hospitality

This visit falls into two parts, concerned respectively with a son for Abraham and the fate of Lot's town of Sodom. It is a scene of courtly oriental hospitality, where the guests are anyway received with deference and generosity. The hotel trade being unknown, and perpetual travelling a way of life, hospitality was all the more important. Even today there is a Jewish saying, 'A sabbath without guests is no sabbath.'

Abraham does them profound reverence, begs them not to pass him by, fetches water for their feet and bids them rest. Then, with the courteous self-deprecation that it is only 'a little bread', serves them the most sumptuous meal we encounter in the Pentateuch (the first five books of the Bible). Only when these preliminaries are complete does business begin.

The question, of course, is who the guests are. They are sometimes singular and sometimes plural. Abraham addresses them as 'My lord', using a title which may be used of the divinity. The eventual editors of the Hebrew Bible regarded it already as a divine title. When it comes to the promise of a son being given, the visitor is suddenly in the singular, and is named with the divine name, 'the Lord', 'Yahweh'. He makes the promise and guarantees it by the same name.

On the other hand, when it comes to setting out for Sodom, there is a split: the two men go off to Sodom and the Lord/Yahweh stays in Abraham's presence. The early writers and artists of the Church saw this wavering as a hint of the Trinity, for the three visitors between them in a way seem make up one Godhead. This is, however, a purely external judgment, not very helpful towards understanding the mystery which will be revealed only in Christ.

The promise

The birth of Isaac is to be the first of a series of births by the powerful intervention of God, and beyond human means, especially the births of Samuel, John the Baptist and Jesus. All these attest the persevering care of God for the people of his promise. Usually it is only the woman who is barren; in this case it is suggested that both parents are too aged for conception. The postponement of the fulfilment of the promise to Abraham is the primary test of his faith. Others will follow.

Bargaining

The bargaining over the salvation of Sodom is again a splendid oriental story. As anyone who has experienced the bazaars of Jerusalem will know, bargaining is a game played with exaggerated courtesy, flattery and more artistry than logic. The game is at least as important as the final settlement, and skilful play merits its reward. So Abraham puts God on his mettle by calling attention to God's impeccable record of justice as judge of the whole world.

At every step he apologizes more profusely, even (or especially) when he is about to make the outrageous suggestion that God intends to destroy the city for the sake of five men. It would be against the rules for God to point out the logical flaw, so he has to give way once again. Each successive plea of Abraham is presented as a final offer!

Abraham must be pleased at the end, when he has whittled the stake down from fifty to ten. The game has been played and won. It makes no odds that the whole game is irrelevant because Abraham cannot even raise the price on which they have agreed! The story is typical of the warm humanity of the Yahwistic tradition, in which even God is prepared to enter so sportingly into the negotiation of a bargain with a human being.

PRAYER

Lord, our relationship with you in prayer need not always be stately and solemn. You show us also that humour and playfulness are gifts of God, and that they can serve your generosity. Grant us confidence and dignity, even when approaching your awesome majesty.

19 Destruction of Sodom

Depravity at Sodom

There are several shocking features in this narrative. The story is told unsparingly. The men of Sodom are blatant in their demands, the angels feisty in their response and defence of Lot. Perhaps the most shocking element is the unhesitating way in which Lot offers his virgin daughters to the lust of the townsfolk. He, at any rate, thinks that their sexual orientation is not directed exclusively to males.

The Hebrews certainly had a detestation of homosexuality; in the law-codes homosexual intercourse is punishable with death. In this they stood in marked contrast to the Hellenistic civilization. The difference is perhaps founded on a difference in the evaluation of marriage, and so of the dignity of women.

In the Bible the importance of the companionship of man and woman in marriage is staked out in the first chapters: companionship between the two partners on equal terms is the reason for the creation of woman: they are to form one 'flesh', or one being. Although legislation on such matters as adultery does not give the woman the same rights as the man, real partnership between man and wife may be seen again and again in the Bible.

Time and again women play a prominent and respected role of their own: Deborah, Jezebel, Athaliah, Judith spring to mind. By contrast in the ancient civilizations of the Near East women are considered much more as sex-objects, under the patronage and leadership of fertility goddesses. In the Hellenistic civilization there is little sign of appreciation of partnership between the sexes; a homosexual relationship, particularly between adult and youth, is considered noble and an important element in a complete education of the young. In the Bible there is a much stronger sense of family, its values, loyalties and obligations, than is obvious in the literature of the surrounding peoples.

But this does nothing to lessen the shock of Lot's offering his daughters to the attentions of his rapacious townspeople. There is a similar spine-chilling offer in Judges 19. The men of Gibeah show the same homosexual lust for a guest, but are fobbed off with the offer of his concubine, whom they abuse to death. The two related stories perhaps help to explain each other: in each case the purpose of the story is to show the absolute sacredness of hospitality. Nothing, even the most horrific of other crimes, may come before its demands.

In the case of the Sodomites the purpose of the story is to show that they were utterly depraved and would stop at nothing. This is the immediate prelude to their annihilation. In New Testament times Sodom is the classic case of refusal to convert; even so, Capernaum suffers by comparison, for 'if the miracles done in you had been done in Sodom, it would have been standing yet' (Matthew 11:23).

The destruction

The extraordinary landscape of the shores of the southern end of the Dead Sea, the traditional location of Sodom, certainly needs explanation. Its grim silence, eerie smell and intense solitude cast a hush over the visitor. The gaunt modern plants for extraction of its salt and other chemicals do nothing to improve this impression. The contrast with the lush vegetation of the south-east corner of the Sea, below where the River Arnon flows in, is all the more striking. The explanation given by the Hebrews was that it could only be the result of divine punishment.

In former years there was a persistent myth that remains of the city existed under the waters of the Dead Sea, awaiting the attentions of archaeologists. The drying-up of the southern end of the sea in recent years has shown that this idea has no foundation.

A further feature of the landscape is the curious isolated, eroded fingers of rock pointing heavenwards among the beetling cliffs to the west of the Sea. Many cultures have a story of punishment for looking back regretfully, for failure to stick decisively by a hard decision. Perhaps the best-known is that of Euridice, the wife of Orpheus, on her journey up from the world of the dead; by looking back she loses her chance of return to life. The feature in the landscape is explained by a similar fault in Lot's wife: was it regret, or only curiosity?

PRAYER

Lord, the annihilation of the wicked city serves me as a reminder of ultimate punishment. I cannot avoid failing you from time to time, but give me always the grace to acknowledge my sin, to repent and return to you in humility and penance.

20 Abraham at Gerar

The story of Abraham and Sarah at Gerar is a doublet of the story about them at the court of Pharaoh in Genesis 12, and again of Isaac and Rebekah at Gerar. In the handing on of stories by oral tradition names easily change. The story of the preservation of the patriarch's wife from absorption into a high-ranked harem comes, then, three times.

This version comes through the Elohistic tradition (see Introduction). It is the earliest full story from this tradition, though there are some traces of it in the story of the covenant in Genesis 15. The name of this tradition derives from the careful use of the divine name 'God' until the special, personal name 'Yahweh/the Lord' has been revealed at the Burning Bush in Exodus 3.

The Elohist stories are told without such immediacy and vividness as those of the Yahwist. The characterization is less lively, and such delightfully 'human' characteristics of God as gave the charm to the story of Abraham's bargaining over Sodom could not occur. Often God appears more distant: instead of the immediacy of contact seen in God appearing and speaking to Abraham, God gives his messages (as in this story) through dreams.

There are also some differences of theological emphasis between the two streams. In general the covenant is more important to the Elohist, whereas the Yahwist regards God's act of grace as pure, unconditional promise. Correspondingly, the Elohist has more care for human morality: in this story the moral implications are more clearly spelled out than in the Yahwist version in Genesis 12, and the clear conscience of Abimelech is made explicit. The author, however, still seems unaware of the legitimacy of Abraham's description of his wife as also his sister, nor does he deem it necessary to excuse Abraham's lack of scruple in abandoning her to the king's attentions. One can only agree with Abimelech's complaint, 'What possessed you to do such a thing?'

Abraham as intercessor

It is interesting that in Abimelech's dream God says that Abraham is a prophet. Abimelech is to ask Abraham to intercede for him. Abraham is the first person in the Bible to be given the role of prophet. It is meant not so much in the normal sense of one who speaks God's will, still less one who foretells the future (not the main task of a prophet). The prophet is primarily a man of God and of prayer, who knows God's will and is close to God, and is therefore—as here—a powerful intercessor.

On several occasions Moses is asked to intercede for the people to avert God's anger. Amos (Amos 7:2) and Jeremiah (Jeremiah 15:11) also intercede for the people. But their intercession is effective only if there is a conversion on the part of the people: 'even if Moses and Samuel pleaded before me, I could not sympathize with this people', says the Lord before the destruction of Jerusalem (Jeremiah 15:1). Intercession for others has always been an important element in the prayer life of Christians.

PRAYER

Lord, the prayer and affection of your friends for their friends is dear to you. Help me to draw to you those in need, in my prayers and in my simple thoughts before you. Prevent me from being self-centred even in my prayers of intercession. Enlarge and widen my love until it becomes as wide as yours.

21

The birth of Isaac

The laughter of Isaac

The birth of Isaac brings the first satisfying fulfilment of God's promise. Ishmael, the slave-girl's son, would have been a poor substitute for a son to Abraham through his wife.

The little verse pronounced by Sarah again puns on the name 'Isaac'. Normally the meaning of a name is expressed by the Bible in a statement by the mother, in such terms as, 'she named the child Ichabod, saying, "The glory is gone from Israel"': In the case of Isaac both Sarah and Abraham have earlier *laughed* ironically at the promise of a child in old age (17:17; 18:12), and one more use of the pun will be Hagar *playing with* Isaac (21:9, the same verb in Hebrew). Now Sarah refreshingly *laughs* for joy at the birth of her son.

The story of the dismissal of Hagar and her son has already been told in chapter 16. As the divine names clearly show, that was a Yahwistic version, and this is the Elohistic tradition. The stories are independent, for according to the ages given to Abraham, Ishmael would be 14 years old at this dismissal, too old to be carried by his mother and left to die under a bush. Each is a story intended to explain the stormy relationship between the two cousinly peoples, Israel and Ishmael, and centred on a well in the southern desert of Judah. Presumably the well is known to both tribes, a meeting-point between them and perhaps a focus-point of argument.

The blessing of water

We shall later come across plenty of arguments over water holes in Jacob's time; such water rights may well have been the focus of argument between the herdsmen of Abraham and Lot, which led to their separation. To dispute over the sources of water is to dispute over the sources of life and wealth.

Water is the key to life in Palestine, and everyone is aware of it. There is an immediate response to such imagery as that of the messianic shepherd, 'By tranquil streams he leads me, to restore my spirit' (Psalm 23). The wonderful vision in Ezekiel 47 of water flowing from the temple, deeper and deeper, causing more abundant and fruitful vegetation as it deepens, is an attractive symbol of God's renewed blessing on his people.

No pilgrim can share the experience of the Bible, who has not come back from the desert, dry and sticky-mouthed, to see the wonder of greenery where the water flows. The Crusader Kingdom, too, fell to thirst, when the army was penned on the Horns of Hattim, within sight of the Lake of Galilee, but unable to reach the water. When Hagar's skin of water was exhausted, there really was nothing to do but leave the child under a bush and weep. And it makes no difference if the skin, hopefully given her by Abraham, has now been exchanged for a plastic container enveloped in polystyrene; when it is empty, you can rely only on God.

The meaning of 'Beersheba'

These two stories of relationships between Abraham and Abimelech are both explanations of the name of Beersheba, then, as now, the major centre in the south of the country. 'Beer' means 'well'. 'Sheba' (like 'bow' in English) has two completely different meanings, either 'to swear an oath' or the number 'seven'. One story is attached to each of these meanings.

PRAYER

Lord, open our eyes to the blessings of nature which you lavish upon us. We are so used to them that we take them for granted. Help us to appreciate them, to harvest them and to thank you for them. Help us also to work that those of your family who lack them may enjoy such benefits too.

22 Abraham's sacrifice

The test of faith

This story gives the ultimate test of Abraham's faith. After he has waited so long for an heir to fulfil the promise God had given him, no sooner had the promise seemed to be on its way to fulfilment than the cup threatens to be dashed from his lips.

The story is sensitively told, centring on the contrast between the merry excitement of the lad as aged father and beloved son set out together on their expedition, and the old man, increasingly heavy-footed in his misery. Even the narrator seems to drag his feet as the dread moment arrives: the narrative advances more and more slowly.

Abraham remains tight-lipped as they set out, not explaining why the wood has been cut, cryptic in his instructions to the two attendants. He tenderly gives the boy only the wood to carry, keeping for himself the knife and the pot of fire, with which the boy might do himself harm. Their affection for each other warms the dialogue between them, with the boy's bouncy inquisitiveness and the father's gentle repudiation of the question. As the moment for sacrifice approaches, there is only a stunned silence between them.

Human sacrifice

The careful narrative brings out to the full the obscenity of a father sacrificing his son. It raises the question how Abraham could accept the order, could even think that this was God's command. Human sacrifice, and precisely child sacrifice, was not unknown in the surrounding nations during the period when these stories were being handed down in Israel.

The tragic story of Jephthah's sacrifice of his young daughter (Judges 11:29–40) shows that it could even be thought to fulfil a vow to Yahweh. The sacrifice of two sons by the rebuilder of Jericho (1 Kings 16:34) in the mid-ninth century is a piece of gruesome superstition: 'Hiel of Bethel rebuilt Jericho. Laying its foundations cost him his eldest son, and erecting its gates cost him his youngest.'

The Law forbids sacrifice to Molech (Leviticus 18:21), also called 'passing through' the fire, some sort of child sacrifice by fire, originating in Phoenicia. There was, then, enough of such practice in the world to make such a dramatic prohibition worthwhile: in Israel this must never occur. So the sacrifice of the son is checked, and the ram is substituted as a victim.

Redemption of the first-born

The same instinct as led to child sacrifice is more humanely expressed in another custom, that of redeeming the first-born. Whatever opens the womb is considered to belong to the Lord. Animals are to be sacrificed, but humans are to be redeemed, bought back at the price of an animal sacrifice. God's ownership of life is expressed by the tabu of blood, the prohibition of consuming blood, which was felt to be the vehicle of life.

Similarly, the redemption of the first-born is, in origin, a repeated acknowledgment that all life belongs to God, and that fertility and the continuance of life are his gift. In Israel it acquires the further dimension of commemoration of the redemption of Israel from captivity and slavery in Egypt (Exodus 13:14–15). The link seems to be the tenth plague, in which the first-born of all Egypt, human and animal, were wiped out.

PRAYER

Lord, you reminded your people constantly by these means that all life is yours, its beginning and its end. Grant me a reverence both for human life and for its reproduction. In all matters of sex we are your honoured agents. Grant that all may see that you are concerned in the moral problems of contraception and euthanasia.

23

The tomb of the patriarchs

The purchase of a plot of land in what was to become the Holy Land is of the highest significance, a landmark for Israel. For generations yet they were to remain nomads, wandering over the border territory between civilization and desert. But now they had their tribal centre, to which they returned each year and where they buried their dead.

The bargain

The story is told with a wit and precision which deserve some explanation. That it is a story of oriental bargaining, when no one means what they say or says what they mean, is obvious enough. But the steely bargaining behind the exaggerated courtesy ('My lord', 'we regard you as a prince of God') depends on knowledge of contemporary law. The people of Hebron are called 'Hittites' and Hittite law-codes of the time hold the clue.

First they try to give him *burial rights*; but Abraham knows that if no land is owned, no rights are granted. Then he tries to buy *part of* the plot; but Ephron knows that if Abraham buys only part, he will not have to take on the citizen obligations (equivalent to our tax obligations). Finally, Ephron, through the courteous suggestion that to a great man like Abraham the sum is paltry indeed, demands a gigantic sum of silver. A last charming touch: even the trees are mentioned as included in the sale, as in every Hittite deed of sale. Abraham finds to his cost that God is a more indulgent partner in a bargain than human merchants!

The memory of Israel

At various points in the stories of the patriarchs it becomes clear that the sacred truths of Israel's God were preserved through human instruments. The stories were handed down as folk-stories are, told round camp fires on winter evenings, by herdsmen swapping stories, by parents soothing their young. Numbers and names of persons and places become uncertain, a village headman grows in importance into a Pharaoh, features of landscape, custom, nomenclature are explained by a story (the name 'Isaac' recurs again and again in his story by the frequent mention of 'laughter', 'smiling', for *Yitzhaq* means 'he will laugh'). It is only the promise of God to Abraham and his constant protection that really matter.

Yet the memory can also be astoundingly correct. As the story of this bargain was handed down for centuries, the story-tellers handed down faithfully the Hittite customs which give life to the story, but had long lost their meaning and relevance in the more sophisticated society after the Exodus. How correct they were, came to light only with the discovery of Hittite legal texts at the beginning of this century. Such discoveries lend confidence to the whole historical basis of our faith.

Hebron today

The town lies in a bowl. In the middle rises majestic the great classical basilica-type hall built by King Herod over the tombs of the patriarchs. The blocks of stone themselves are magnificent, the largest being over seven metres long and nearly two metres high. The aura of reverence from three faiths, Jewish, Christian and Muslim, for the tombs within is almost tangible. If places can be sanctified by the expression of faith in centuries of prayer and pilgrimage, here is one of the most sacred. It has a continuous tradition of over three millennia, as pilgrims remember the choice by God of three generations of almost nameless nomads to be the founders of his people.

PRAYER

Lord, you granted a place where the fathers of your people might rest. Grant that as we wait for the resurrection on the last day we may rest in your arms as your chosen ones.

24 The marriage of Isaac

The mission to Aram Naharaim

Abraham's two thrusts behind this mission are the promise of the land and the continuance of the line. The promise of the land means that his son must at all costs stay in the land which God has given them. The continuance of the line is probably more a primitive tribal instinct than motivated by any religious or theological reason. Abraham is determined to keep the stock pure. This may be in order to avoid contamination with the religions of the land, but these have so far played no part in any of the stories, and we do not know how they were conceived. In later times, at the settlement in Canaan after their period in Egypt, and at the return to Judea from exile in Babylon, intermarriage and all contact with the local people was strictly prohibited. Cultic and religious contamination was a real danger.

A delightful portrait of Rebekah and her family emerges. Rebekah is quick and eager in serving her guest, but gives him plenty of time. She goes beyond his request, not only offering to water the camels, but even inviting him to stay the night. To remove all hesitation (and the guest quite properly waits for confirmation from the head of the family), Laban shows the same eagerness in running out to repeat the invitation. It is perhaps not too cynical to remark that he has already noticed the ring and the bracelets his sister is wearing, pledge of further presents to come!

God's covenant love

The envoy's immediate success, the fulfilment of the sign he demands, the warm welcome he receives, and the willingness of the bride-to-be are all signs that the hand of God is there. The principal emphasis, however, is on the sign and its fulfilment. This is repeated several times in the course of the narrative, and stressed by the exact way in which the signs are fulfilled. It is an expression of God's fidelity to his covenant, 'his faithful love for my master' (verse 27).

This is the faithful love which echoes down the Bible, the guarantee of his care. One of the fullest explanations of it is given in Exodus 34: after the people have been unfaithful by idolatry of the Golden Calf, Yahweh reveals the meaning of his name, as faithful love and forgiveness. But it is the basis of the whole of the covenant relationship, often spoken (the refrain of many of the psalms, such as Psalm 136, 'for his great love is without end'), but more often unspoken and presumed.

There is a certain amount of confusion about Rebekah's parentage. In a couple of passages she is described as the daughter of Nahor, so niece to Abraham. Elsewhere she is daughter of Bethuel, son of Nahor, so grand-niece to Abraham. By now, however, the head of the family is her brother Laban. Family law at the time prescribed that if the head of a family was father to a girl he could arrange her marriage without consent. If, as in this case, the head of the family is brother to the girl, he must ask her consent. This Laban duly does. As so often, oriental courtesy cloaks the hard realities of business: the 'rich presents to her brother' are of course the bride-price.

PRAYER

Father, in your love for your people you watch over each detail of their existence. Just as you assured the continuance of Abraham's line in the Old Covenant, so you assure the continuance of your Church in the New Covenant. Let us rest in this love, confident that we rely on your strength, not our own.

25 The death of Abraham

Abraham was laid to rest in the tomb he had bought for his wife. His immense catafalque is still revered at Hebron, in Herod's impressive building, as the tomb of the Friend of God. Since the massacre there in 1994 of Moslem worshippers by an Israeli fanatic, it is not only hallowed by centuries of prayer but also a reminder of human intolerance even (or especially) in the name of religion.

Belief in immortality or eternal life, the hope of Christians, comes at the end of a long development. In the early centuries, as we see here in the case of Abraham, it was thought that the dead person was simply 'gathered to his people', falling back into the tribal corporate personality; it is the tribal, not the personal, identity which is paramount. This persists until David, who mourns for his infant son, the fruit of his adultery with Bathsheba, 'I shall go to him, but he cannot come back to me' (2 Samuel 12:23). The son has been gathered to his ancestors, and David can only hope to join him.

Sheol

Later on we find the concept of Sheol, a dark, dusty and unhappy place below the earth, where the spirits of the dead endure a lifeless and listless existence. For the true Israelite the ultimate horror of this is separation from God, inability even to praise him: 'Can shadows rise up to praise you? Do they speak in the grave of your faithful love?' (Psalm 88:10). There the great kings of the earth sit lifeless on their thrones, rising to greet a new arrival, 'So, you too are now as weak as we are!' (Isaiah 14:10).

Job could not stomach this picture. Job was nothing if not stubborn. He refused to accept that the God who was his protector would leave him for ever unsatisfied in Sheol. Some day this same God who afflicts him will also vindicate him, so that Job will be close to him and in his company: 'I know that I have a living Defender; after my awakening he will set me close to him, and from my flesh I shall look on God' (Job 19:25).

This is much the same attitude as that expressed by Jesus when the Sadducees try to catch him out with their riddle about the woman who had been married seven times: Jesus replies that God said, 'I am the God of Abraham, Isaac and Jacob'—that is, I am still their God. Abraham, Isaac and Jacob are bonded to him permanently, and have not been lost to him. Even though they are dead, he will not forsake them. This is what is meant by the insistence that he 'is the God not of the dead but of the living' (Mark 12:27): for him and in him, all are alive.

To live for ever

It was not till the wars in defence of the Jewish way of life during the Maccabean persecution, in the second century BC, that the conviction is evident that the just will rise again at the end of time. The martyrs who have died in defence of Judaism will rise 'to live again for ever' (2 Maccabees 7:9). This general resurrection is to be at the end of time.

The staggering shock of the resurrection of Jesus, which left the women witless and bemused, was that it should occur suddenly, within time and without bringing time to an end. The Christian belief is that those who are in Christ will join him in this transformed life. This is beautifully expressed—bringing the idea full circle—by the idea of the descent into hell. Whatever else this means, it means that Christ fetches into his risen life the patriarchs already dead, and languishing in Sheol. The Byzantine mosaics picture this as the risen Christ drawing Adam or Abraham by the hand from the tomb.

PRAYER

God of Abraham, Isaac and Jacob, you are our hope of eternal happiness. As Abraham died he could not envisage what his faithful protector had in store for him. No more can we understand what no eye has seen, no ear has heard. Grant us to wait in patience and confidence for your loving will to be done, secure in your eternal embrace.

26 Esau and Jacob are born

Isaac and the promise

Isaac remains a shadowy figure, the least substantial of the three great patriarchs, overshadowed by Abraham and Jacob. The only story in which he features centrally is the story about the dispute over the wells. Otherwise he features as the recipient of the wife (Rebekah) arranged by his father, as the almost-cuckolded husband (a story he shares with his father, Abraham), and the old man deceived by his scheming wife and younger son. Yet his importance is that he too is the recipient of God's promise.

Just as Abraham's wife was barren, and the choice of God was emphasized by the miraculous birth of their son, so too with Rebekah. She is barren, and the power of God is shown by her conception—through God's special intervention in answer to Isaac's prayer—of the next generation which furthers the promise.

The traditional twelve tribes came to be regarded as all descended from the twelve sons of Jacob, although historically the origin of the tribes may have been very diverse. Many historians hold that some came from Egypt with Moses and entered the Promised Land with the main body. Some joined Moses' group during the desert wanderings. Some never went down to Egypt.

The central thread is that all committed themselves to worship of Moses' God, and to the covenant made with him, and so became spiritually children of Jacob. We have seen that in these ancient stories, handed down for generations by word of mouth, the names sometimes get mixed. The same principle would allow that Isaac, the most shadowy figure, could be historically the most ancient of the trio.

The twins

The stories of the twins revolve round the history of the tribes descended from them, and round the meaning of their names. Historically the basic element is the rivalry between the tribes descended from them. Edom, in the highlands on the eastern side of the Jordan, refused to allow the Hebrews to pass through their territory on their journey into the Promised Land, forcing them to make a long detour.

In later centuries, when Israel expanded during the reign of King David, Edom waged intermittent war against Israel. David conquered Edom, but under Solomon they broke free. The ding-dong battle continued for generations, and this is reflected in the rivalry of the twin ancestors.

But behind all the historical allusion is the hard contrast between the purposes of the two. This is the real point of the story. Esau is materialistic and devil-may-care ('That was all Esau cared about his birthright'), while Jacob concentrates all his efforts on the succession. He is the fitting holder of the promise of God.

Puns

There is a play here on the meaning of several words. The mentions of 'red' reflect Edom, for which the Hebrew is *adom* (a light *a*, easily interchangeable with *e*, especially in Hebrew, where the consonants are all-important and the vowels less so)—thus both the red hair and the red stew. In fact 'hair' provides another pun: the Hebrew for 'hair' is *se'ir*, which is also the name for one of the main districts of Edom.

Various parts of the stories pun on the name Jacob. The Hebrew form of the name is *Ya'aqob*. This is considered close enough to *'aqeb* (=heel) to justify the detail of Jacob grasping his brother's heel at birth. It is also punned several times with *'aqab* (=supplant) in the elements of the two stories which show Jacob supplanting his brother. Both of these explanations are in fact probably incorrect, reflecting the Hebrew love of giving meaning to names. The original form of the name may well have been *Ya'aqob-El*, which means 'May the god El protect!' The name occurs in this form in the ancient land of Canaan, later to become Israel.

PRAYER

O God, it is good to see that even within your chosen family squabbles and sibling rivalry could occur. Help us to work always to avoid such rivalry and to learn generosity and forgiveness especially towards those naturally closest to us.

27

Isaac at Gerar

The promise to Isaac

The chief importance about the patriarchs is the promises they received. So the first story in which Isaac plays a leading role is the story of the renewal to him of the promise made to Abraham. It is the same promise as Abraham received in Genesis 12 and 22, but acquires a new anchor-hold from its repetition to Isaac.

The patriarch's wife endangered

We have encountered this story already twice in the history of Abraham. On the first occasion the man involved was Pharaoh, king of Egypt, on the second Abimelech, king of Gerar, as here. The story serves to show God's careful and repeated protection of his people, and more especially of the succession and inheritance of the promise. The details vary slightly in each case. On this occasion we have the clever little touch of the pun on Isaac's name: in Hebrew the name is *Yitzhaq*; when Abimelech looks out of the window and sees Isaac fondling his wife Rebekah, Isaac is *metzaheq*.

It is not easy for an impoverished nomad to withstand the advances of the ruler of the land—no doubt the bride-price would be astronomical!—but God will not allow his purposes to be deflected. The story contains quite a paradoxical contrast between the two men. The Philistine king keeps carefully to his high moral principles (high, that is, within the contemporary conventions of royal harems), and even insists on avoiding the responsibility for a possible fault of one of his followers. Isaac, on the other hand, thinks only of his own skin, or possibly even the advantages of selling his wife, leaving to God any care for fulfilling the promise! God shows considerably more care for his promise than does the beneficiary of it.

Gerar

The king of Gerar is described as a Philistine. But the Philistines arrived on the coast of Palestine (which drew its name from them) only after 1198, whereas this story is several centuries earlier. Nevertheless, 'Philistine' remains a handy designation of the area, the very fertile coastal strip along the eastern shore of the Mediterranean, enriched with sandy soil from the Nile Delta, and today the source of much soft fruit in European markets (Jaffa Oranges!). Gerar has been identified with a strong fortress found to the extreme south-east of this territory, on the borders of the fertile land and the fiercely arid desert of the Negeb.

This is indeed the Isaac country. Even today in time of drought the nomads of the desert migrate with their flocks of sheep and goats to the more fertile areas on the edge of the desert in search of pasture and water. In this search Abraham had gone to Egypt (and so later would Jacob), and had the same experience as Isaac of risking the loss of his wife into the ruler's harem. This was simply a move to a different border of the nomad area.

This story brings us also a notable little advance: for the first time the nomad begins to sow and reap crops. This is the first indication of a transfer to a sedentary way of life, and beginning to embrace agriculture.

PRAYER

O God, you protect us from all dangers, looking after our interests more zealously than we do ourselves. Help me to overcome my carelessness and indifference to your will, and keep me single-minded in your service.

28
The wells between Gerar and Beersheba

Disputes over wells

The circumstances of the end of Isaac's stay in Gerar are quite different from those of Abraham's departure from Egypt and Gerar after the incidents of his endangered wife. In the case of Abraham he is asked to leave because of the fear of divine displeasure. In the case of Isaac it is envy from the local inhabitants at his increase of wealth. Isaac is already developing into a power in the land, which Abraham never was.

We have, however, seen before (chapter 13) how disputes broke out between herdsmen in that sparse land where resources are so much at a premium. On the edge of the Negeb water is the most valuable commodity of all, and a well is a prized possession. In this case the wells of a previous generation could have been blocked up either to hide them or out of deliberate, malicious sabotage.

In the Hebrew fashion, the stories are also related to the name of the wells. The Hebrew word *'esek* means 'quarrel' and *sitnah* means 'accusation'. There is certainly plenty of room for both in this ugly situation. Abraham had staked out a certain claim to ownership, or at least use, of the land by digging the wells. The local inhabitants had responded, perhaps on Abraham's departure, by blocking the wells. Now Isaac is growing in wealth and attempts to settle at least on the borders of territory claimed by Abimelech.

He withdraws only a little, settling still in the Valley of Gerar. These are not the preparations for peaceful coexistence. One can almost sense the relief when Isaac finally moves off and settles with more 'breadth', both physical and spiritual, at *Rehovoth*. The name means 'wide open spaces', and by itself conjures up the rolling open plains between Beersheba and the coastal strip.

Renewal of the promise

In his instructions to go to Gerar God had already alluded to the promise to Abraham. Now the promise is explicitly and formally renewed, with a little verse or rhythmical speech—and verse is always more easily remembered and recited than prose.

God still needs to identify himself. In the Near East there were many gods, gods of local shrines, of wells, of striking features of the landscape, of fertility, of storms. One class of gods, especially in the mobile situation of nomads, was personal gods. Groups of inscriptions have been found, stemming from nomadic tribes similar to those of Isaac and Abraham, dedicated 'To the God of [a certain person]'. This God, originally revered by that one person, has obviously become a tribal deity. To Isaac this still largely unknown God now makes the link by identifying himself as the same God who had promised his protection to Abraham.

It should not be shocking that other divinities were revered in the same way as the God of Abraham. The God of Abraham is the true God, but does it follow that the others were all false? Other tribes, too, were searching. They committed themselves to a deity who was an approximation more or less close to the true God, perhaps sometimes close, perhaps sometimes distanced by the barbarity of beliefs and practices associated with the cult. Did such worshippers merely *invent* their gods, in sharp contrast to the revelation *received* by Abraham, Isaac and Jacob? Or were the other tribes too guided by the loving hand of the true God, to arrive at least at some approximation to true insight and true belief?

PRAYER

God of Abraham, Isaac and Jacob, you showed yourself to our ancestors in faith, and guided them painstakingly over centuries to the fulness of your revelation in Christ. Help us also to see your guiding hand in other religions and cultures which are searching for you.

Alliance with Abimelech

The alliance

This story seems to give an explanation both of the name of the well and the town centred upon it, and of relationships between the people of Isaac and of Abimelech. The Hebrew word *beer* means 'well', and *sheba'* means 'oath', giving the combination the meaning 'well of the oath'. The oath between these two ancestors of peoples seems the obvious candidate to explain it.

The town of Beersheba, even today, is an important centre on the northern edge of the Negeb for the Arabs of that region. It stands at the important crossroads of the route running from the north to the Red Sea and the Indian Ocean, and the caravan route across the north of the Negeb to the Mediterranean. Through the Israeli irrigation projects, cultivation has advanced considerably in the last two decades; but at least until then the surrounding culture was still at the same stage as that of Isaac, nomads beginning to change from an economy of flocks to agriculture.

It is less easy to see just what long-term alliance is commemorated. It is inaccurate to consider Abimelech a representative of the Philistines, for they arrived on the coast of Palestine only some centuries later. Nor, to judge from David's freebooting activities when he was in the service of the Philistines, were relations between the Philistines and the inhabitants of the Negeb good; David was sent out raiding all over the territory, with the intention of making him unpopular with his own people (1 Samuel 27:8–12: but he was in fact far too clever to play into the hands of the Philistines). So alliance between the Philistines and the people of Isaac can hardly be what the writer has in mind here.

The promise begins to be fulfilled

However, it is impressive to see how Isaac's status has changed. While Abraham was chased away from Gerar with a gift, Isaac receives an official embassy, consisting of the king with his adviser and his general. Isaac can even afford.to challenge them, somewhat truculently. In reply the envoys have to point out (as was often done in the preamble to ancient treaties) the benefits they have conferred. Control of this major centre on the caravan routes, and of at least two other watering-points has clearly given Isaac a firm position and a measure of confidence and power. The promise of possession of the land is beginning to burgeon.

Esau's Hittite wives

This little notice, typical of the Priestly writer (see Introduction), reflects the concern, even at this early stage, with the worries of subsequent history. Esau's two Hittite wives would have been particularly alarming to the Priestly writer, because of the foreign practices and worship that foreign wives who did not worship the God of Israel had introduced in the course of history.

This had been a problem especially at three periods: first at the entry of the Israelites into Canaan under Joshua, when all contact with the people of the land had been rigorously forbidden, let alone intermarriage.

The second danger came from Solomon's foreign wives, who were considered responsible for the intermingling of their own idolatry and foreign cults; it was through such intermarriage that the idolatrous cults were introduced which the prophets so abhorred (Deuteronomy 7;1–4).

The third period was at the return of Israel from exile in Babylon, when those remnants who had not been exiled, the 'people of the land', had embraced many superstitions. Marriage between them and the returning exiles was again severely forbidden, and such marriages were dissolved by Ezra's legislation (Ezra 9–10). The Priestly writer sees Esau's foreign spouses as a foretaste of this unfaithfulness.

PRAYER

Lord God, your promises are fulfilled in your own good time, sometimes gradually and seemingly only in part. Grant me the openness to see your care in all the events of life, and the patience to wait for your good time.

30 Jacob obtains Isaac's blessing by fraud

Suspense

This well-loved story stirs many emotions in the modern reader. On the dramatic level the suspense is wonderfully achieved. Deprived of sight, poor old Isaac uses all his other senses.

First the suspense is heightened by his still-sharp hearing: he can distinguish the tones of the voices of his sons, and becomes suspicious. Then touch partially allays the suspicion, as he feels the hairy arms (note the pun again on 'hair' and *se'ir*, as in Genesis 25). Taste is somewhat neglected by the pair of plotters, in the justified hope that he will not be able to distinguish between a wild goat (possibly an ibex, as they are common in the area) and a goat from the flock.

Finally the sense of smell comes into play, not as part of the recognition, but as part of the blessing conferred on Jacob: the blessing of the fertile field and the 'homestead farm' corresponds to what we already know about Jacob. It is sharply at variance with the wild blessing for the wild man who is Esau. The suspense carries on through each of the senses, for any could have given away the plot. Even beyond this the suspense remains: can the blessing be revoked and exchanged for a curse for the deception? Esau knows all too well that it cannot be, and that he must be content with a secondary blessing.

Chief among the emotions aroused must be pity for old, blind Isaac and for the duped elder son. This will be balanced by indignation at the unjust trickery of Isaac's wife and younger son, coupled with astonishment that this can be permitted by God and even put forward—by implication—as praiseworthy. St Augustine was famously reduced to calling it 'not a lie but a mystery'; it might have been fairer to admit that it was both of these!

The ancient story-teller or reader would have reacted differently, and that on two counts, one theological and one moral. Of paramount importance in Israel was God's promise. Nothing may be put before this, for it is at the heart of Israel's existence. We have already experienced the promise to Abraham and to Isaac, and later in the history this is to be extended to the whole people by God's promise on Sinai to take them to himself as his own special people. To inherit this promise is the secret of Israel's existence, and surely to gain God's blessing anything goes?

The story shows once more, and not for the last time, God's choice of the younger son. He chooses whom he will, and his sovereign will can be expressed even by behaviour such as this.

Morality

Commentators often remark that the morality of this story is 'primitive' or 'undeveloped'. Lying within the family is particularly offensive, and using the handicaps of the elderly against them makes this worse. Infidelity to a son and a brother, particularly as he is obediently indulging his aged father's whim, further increases the offence. The moral problem is perhaps exacerbated for us by their brazenness: Rebekah is happy to accept any curse evoked by the failure of the scheme, and Jacob has the gall to say that Yahweh *your* God made things go well for him. And yet God is seen as approving all this, allowing the dastardly ruse to succeed, conniving in it and conferring his blessing!

The truth is that the standards of judgment are simply different. This story betrays an attitude that a clever ruse is automatically praiseworthy. In a culture where survival depends on quick wit, the pair would be praised for their cleverness. I have myself experienced (and nearly suffered) the same in recent encounters with people of the desert.

PRAYER

Lord, you educated your people slowly and painfully. You would not have us approve everything they did. Grant me the burning desire for the grasp of your promises, but also respect for personal and family values.

Isaac sends Jacob to Laban

Jacob's mission

This account, characteristic of the Priestly writer, gives a far less colourful version of Isaac's blessing on Jacob. It is shorn of the drama and deception of the Yahwistic version in chapter 27. There is no sign of the deception of Isaac or the ousting of Esau. Simply Jacob is sent back by his father to their ancestral territory to keep the stock pure by finding a wife there—just as, in the previous generation, Abraham had sent his envoy back to find a wife for Isaac himself. It is the preparation for the stories of Jacob's service of his uncle Laban, and his laborious winning of a wife.

The contrast with Esau comes calmly in the next paragraph, centred on the Hittite or Canaanite wives mentioned at the end of Genesis 26 (the appellations 'Hittite' and 'Canaanite' are, of course, different; the point is that they are local women, not of the stock of Abraham). In this story Esau does his best to right the situation, by marrying the granddaughter of Abraham. His own wild ethnic quality is still preserved because she is the daughter of Ishmael, 'a wild donkey of a man, his hand against every man, and every man's hand against him' (Genesis 16:12), representing the warlike tribes of the desert of the Negeb. We are still reminded of the strife between the settled Israelites and their wilder neighbours to the south and east.

El Shaddai

In the stories of Genesis God is known by several names. 'El' is the general word for 'God', which comes in a plural form as 'Elohim'. 'El Shaddai' may mean either 'God of the mountains' or 'God of the open spaces', according to whether the second word is taken from a Hebrew or a Mesopotamian root.

In Genesis 14 Melchizedek was called 'a priest of El Elyon'; this title was perhaps the one used at Jerusalem. Similarly El Shaddai seems to be linked to the sanctuary at Hebron. We have also, of course, met the name 'Yahweh' already being used, though the story of this name being revealed to Moses in Egypt will be told some time later.

This variety of names for God reflects the richness of the religious tradition. The names presumably originally represented different gods, worshipped at different shrines or for different properties. It is common for primitive religions to revere many gods, each connected with a special property or position. The sphere of the god is comparatively narrow. Thus God is revealed to Abraham as his personal protector and the protector of his clan, who will make his descendants like the stars of the heavens or the sand on the seashore.

There is at first no thought of the relationship of these deities to a wider world and to one another. It is only with the progress of religion and revelation that it is perceived that a multiplicity of gods is a contradiction in terms. The very conception of 'God', as it is understood in the Hebrew and Christian tradition, involves uniqueness.

It is therefore a significant step forward in God's gift of knowledge when it becomes clear that all these 'gods', first known as local or particularized deities, point in fact to the one God. Some aspects of the way in which they are conceived may be incompatible with the true conception of God—a god cannot be God who calls for the sacrifice of children. But in so far as they are genuinely divine, these deities are all manifestations, more or less complete, of the one God.

There are many ways of coming to the knowledge of God; some of these are bound to be tentative and only partially successful. The variety of names for God is a memorial of these tentative endeavours.

PRAYER
Lord God, you allow us to come to knowledge of yourself in myriad ways. Grant me a true knowledge of yourself. Protect me from the limitations of my knowledge and conception of you, and save me from idolatry in any form. Guide me into the full splendour of the vision of you as you really are.

GENESIS 28:10–22
Jacob's dream

As Jacob is on his way to find a wife and continue the line he is given a renewed promise by God. God offers the self-identification of 'the God of Abraham your father and the God of Jacob'. This God is the ancestral deity, who had promised to protect the fathers of the tribe, but had still not given them his personal name. His promise will be an assurance to Jacob particularly in the long testing time he is to endure, and a guarantee of the eventual return to the Promised Land.

Ancient symbols

This is an alluringly primitive story, with a rich background in the religious symbolism of the Near East. It seems basically to be the cult-legend of Bethel. It would have been preserved and handed down to explain why Bethel was revered as a meeting-place with God. This became particularly important after the division of the two kingdoms at the death of Solomon, for Bethel became the national sanctuary of the northern kingdom. Political and religious independence must go hand in hand; it would have been difficult for the northerners to retain their self-respect if they had had to make the pilgrimage to Jerusalem to worship God.

To a certain extent Bethel was the symbol of the division within God's people. It is therefore remarkable that this narrative survived the denunciations of the sanctuary at Bethel made by the prophets Amos and Hosea. 'Go to Bethel and sin!' declares Amos (Amos 4:4). Hosea puns on the name, calling it 'Beth-Aven' ('house of evil') instead of Bethel ('house of God'): 'though you, Israel, play the whore, there is no need for Judah to sin too; do not go up to Beth-Aven' (Hosea 4:15).

The stone which forms Jacob's pillow is religiously dubious as well. Sacred stones were forbidden to Israel, as objects of superstition. They could easily engender too materialistic a notion of God. But they were common among Israel's neighbours. Islam has the *ka'aba* stone at Mecca; primitive British rites had such phenomena as

Stonehenge and Avebury Circle. At the end of the story Jacob sets up his pillow as a pillar or orthostat, and consecrates it by anointing it with oil. This too is a remarkable survival in the story, in the teeth of the prohibition of sacred stones in the Law (Exodus 23:24). Jacob makes it the witness and guarantee of his commitment to God if God blesses him by fulfilling his prayer.

The 'ladder' too has ancient religious significance: it is really not so much what is indicated by a modern ladder as a stairway leading up to heaven, like the stairways of the ancient Mesopotamian ziggurats. It was at the top of these great, formal stairways that the meeting with the divinity was envisaged; so they were the stairway to heaven. Ziggurats were pilloried in the story of the tower of Babel as unsuccessful, human ways of trying to reach God. But again, this piece of lore remains to express the divine promise given to Jacob. However, in this case the stairway is built not by human effort but by God's own approach to Jacob. The angels are the sign of his communication, for 'angel' means 'messenger'.

The Christian dimension

For Christians the story has the additional dimension provided through the allusion to it by the Johannine Jesus, 'In all truth I tell you, you will see heaven open and the angels of God ascending and descending on the Son of man' (John 1:51). 'Jacob's Ladder' is only a foretaste of a fuller opening of the heavens. Jesus is seen as being the perfect means of communication with God, the place where the fulness of revelation occurs, giving those to whom he reveals himself access to the secrets of God's nature.

PRAYER

Lord God, this stairway is already the pledge of your openness and your gift of yourself to your people. You wish such communication to remain open always. Ensure that I do not cut myself off or hide from you, but always receive your message with gratitude and joy.

Jacob and Rachel

33

The meeting of Jacob and Rachel

The meeting of Jacob with Rachel is very similar to that of Abraham's envoy with Rebekah. The remarkable factor about both meetings is the freedom of the girl. In the Rebekah story she comes on her own to fetch water and converses freely and easily with the stranger; perhaps this is helped by a certain seniority of the stranger!

In the Rachel story the girl is moving freely around with her father's flocks among the male shepherds. When the young couple fall in love at first sight, they kiss each other openly—before Jacob has told her that he is her first cousin! Then the warmth of the family greetings is delightful: Jacob bursting into tears, everyone running to tell the news, kisses all round and the proud welcome, 'You are indeed my bone and my flesh!' It is an attractive scene of the exile's homecoming.

The romantic atmosphere is heightened by the impression that Jacob does heroic feats for his lady-love. The most obvious meaning of the shepherds' statement that they cannot move the stone till all are assembled is that the stone is so large that it requires all hands. Yet Jacob performs it single-handed. The same charm continues in his working for seven years, 'and they seemed to him like a few days'.

Beneath all this family rejoicing is the message that God's promise is working itself out. God is looking after the stock of Abraham in accordance with his promise, and ensuring that all goes smoothly.

Jacob's marriages

When it comes to the marriage, however, Uncle Laban shows himself a match for the cunning shown by Nephew Jacob towards his father and brother. The bride-price, consisting in seven years' labour, is surely uncomfortably high, once Laban knows that Jacob is head over heels in love. He then operates the trickery with Leah, exploiting the custom of keeping the bride veiled till evening, when it was presumably too dark to distinguish the two.

Incidentally we do not really know the quality of Leah's eyes complimented by Jacob. The meaning of the Hebrew word is not clearly known, so KJV chooses 'tender', NIV has 'weak' or 'delicate', NRSV and NJB 'lovely'. Is Jacob being gallant to the less favoured sister?

To justify his conduct Laban produces a custom that in his society the elder sister is always married first, seemingly without any embarrassment that this is the first time Jacob has heard about it. We can only give Laban the benefit of the doubt; we have no evidence to corroborate his claim!

In the event the impression is given that Jacob married Rachel immediately, and worked his bride-price of seven years for her subsequently. Each of them presents him also with a slave-girl, who would become a wife of lower status. The stage is set for the twelve sons who will be born to Jacob, and will be regarded as the ancestors of the classic twelve tribes. This is the last time we hear of such luxuriant polygamy in Israel, though Gideon had many wives (and seventy sons, Judges 8:30), perhaps exercising the privilege of royalty.

The Assyrian law-codes were stricter: a man might have only one wife, though one concubine also was permitted. Indeed, if the wife was barren, she could present him with a concubine, as occurred in the case of Abraham: Sarah presented him with her slave-girl Hagar. In the patriarchal stories jealousy and rivalry always seem to have followed, if not among the wives, at least among their children.

PRAYER

Father, you are the model of all fatherhood and the key to all family values. Grant joy to all Christian families. May all treasure the relationships you have given them, responding to one another with your loving generosity.

34
Jacob's children

Biblical genealogies

As we have seen on the occasion of various lists of descendants, such as those of Noah, the purpose of these biblical genealogies is not to tell the stories of births in the remote past, but to explain the present structure and division of peoples and their interrelationships.

An important part in this is always played by names, for names reflect and express the nature of the person or object named. By naming the beasts, Adam prescribed their nature and their function in human intercourse. In the same way the Hebrews felt that personal names must always have significance, and somehow reflect the nature of the bearer, often even through rather improbable puns on the sound of the name in Hebrew.

We have seen this in the various wordplays on the names of Isaac and Jacob. These puns are normally expressed in the form of an exclamation by the mother at birth. 'Said' and 'meant' are often interchangeable, so that 'for she said...' is an obvious way of explaining the meaning of a name, as though it were 'what she meant by this is...'

The mothers of Jacob's sons

The chapter is bound together by the theme of the jealousy and rivalry between the two wives—and the use of their slave-girls in ensuring Jacob's affection. The meaning of the names is chiefly attached to this. One sub-theme is the ancient belief that mandrakes have aphrodisiac or fertility properties. Here again the story is built on wordplay: the name for mandrakes is related to the word for love, and they have been called 'love-apples'.

The acrid commercial rivalry which goes on between the two sisters over the sale and payment for this aphrodisiac centres round the name of the son born. 'Issachar' can be related to the Hebrew word meaning 'reward' or 'hire'. But, despite the intrusion of this piece of superstition, the account is dominated by a clear awareness that God is responsible for fertility and birth. God is the author of life and increase, and this is reflected in most of the names. It is especially part of his realization of his promise to Abraham, Isaac and Jacob: the peopling of the tribes descended from Jacob is being prepared.

Unity in worship

As has already been pointed out (in note 26), the descent of the twelve tribes from the actual sons of Jacob is more a statement of their religious unity and solidarity at a certain point in later history than it is a reflection of the actual historical origin of the tribes.

This is the more remarkable in that their politico-military history shows a very patchy response: when united action was required against an invader, as in the days of Deborah (Judges 5), several of the tribes failed to send help. The basis of unity between the tribes was their worship of Yahweh and their commitment to him as their defender (Judges 23).

A table of the names and the meaning given to them may be helpful. Further details would only be confusing, partly through the complications of Hebrew grammar, and partly because some of the meanings and the roots of the words are forced.

SON	MOTHER	MEANING
Reuben	Leah	has seen my sorrow
Simeon	Leah	has heard
Levi	Leah	he unites
Judah	Leah	I shall praise
Dan	Bilhah	does justice to me
Naphtali	Bilhah	I have fought
Gad	Zilpah	good fortune
Asher	Zilpah	blessed
Issachar	Leah	will reward
Zebulun	Leah	give presents
Joseph	Rachel	will add
Benjamin	Rachel	son of sorrow (35:16–20)

PRAYER

Father, you brought the tribes together to form your loyal people. Grant a return to unity among your people in this day, an ability to overcome rivalry, dissension and jealousy, and a determination to work together as your children.

35 How Jacob became rich

Jacob is back to his trickery again! This is another story of cunning, like that of the ousting of Esau, only without at least any overt dishonesty—merely sharp practice, or agricultural business competition! The real wit of the story consists in the fact that both parties are highly competitive and are known beforehand to rely on their wits; this is going to be a real competition.

It starts with what appears to be a case of oriental bargaining, where the hard facts are concealed under a thick layer of oily courtesy, and nobody is so coarse as to mention them. Jacob begins by pointing out ('you know how long I have worked for you') that he has worked off his fourteen years of bride-price and now needs to think of his own interests. Laban presses him to stay, with some generous flattery. God is doubly involved on Jacob's side: not only has God blessed Laban because of Jacob, but Laban has been divinely informed of the fact.

This is followed by an even more generous offer. So, having an initial advantage, Jacob changes his tune and protests that he wouldn't dream of accepting any wages. Secure in the knowledge of his little trick, he can appear to offer to work for nothing. While appearing magnanimously to accept as his wages only the mutant misfits of the flock, he in fact makes sure that the apparently mutant misfits are the cream of the flock. This is done by means of sympathetic magic.

There are two presuppositions to Jacob's trickery: first, that the black sheep and the speckled goats are regarded as the runts of the flock, and second, that the colour of the offspring of the flock is determined by whatever the dam was looking at during the mating. Laban presumably thinks (as do modern theorists!) that the colour of the offspring follows that of the parents. With his usual niggardliness, he removes all the animals which should make the dams produce offspring which will fall to Jacob.

Uncle and nephew clearly know each other well, and uncle thinks he has got the measure of nephew. He takes his own flocks three days' journey away, fondly imagining that he is ensuring against any hanky-panky, but in fact giving Jacob plenty of opportunity to operate unheeded. Jacob, however, is too clever for his uncle, and overrides these precautions by his sympathetic magic. By his trick with the coloured strips of wood he makes sure that the sturdier strains produce offspring of the colours that fall to him. (It is, of course, possible that Laban has the same genetic theories as Jacob, but simply imagines that Jacob will be unable to produce the right conditions of stripy background.)

There is a further delicious turn to the story, in that 'poplar' (*libneh* in Hebrew) and the 'white stripes' (*lebanoth*) both provide a play on words with Laban's name. It is as though Laban himself contributes to his own discomfiture.

PRAYER

Lord, we are often faced with difficult decisions about business morality. These are frequently more complicated than this canny agricultural bargaining. Help me to understand the issues and principles involved, no matter how tortuous the morality. Grant me always to be not naive, but honest in my business dealings. Save me from taking unfair advantage of others in exploiting their weaknesses.

36

Jacob's flight

Here we find ourselves witnessing a really ugly family row or series of rows. Learned commentators tend to insist on logical consistency throughout, and so find themselves compelled to suggest that many verses (for example, the inconsistent vision of verse 29) are later interpolations. An alternative method is to interpret the story with the dramatic inconsistencies of a family row. The main episodes are:

1. Laban's sons accuse Jacob of profiteering at their father's expense. This is not far from the truth, but is not exactly true either. Laban had agreed to the terms of the bargain, and had taken good care that it should be to his advantage.

2. Jacob accuses his father-in-law, their father, to his wives. He claims that Laban has tricked him, changing his wages ten times over. This may or may not be true, but at least it is a different version of events from that of the previous chapter. Jacob also recounts a message from God (or the Angel of God) that he should set off home, coupled with the story of a dream.

3. The wives are so alienated from their father that they accuse him of selling them and swallowing up the money he got for them. This sounds very biased. Accepting a bride-price was standard practice, and could hardly be described as sale. Had he really swallowed up the money? In Mesopotamian law he was allowed the use of and interest on the money, though the capital came to the women on his death. For good measure the daughters steal their father's 'household idols', which are not necessarily formally idolatrous, but in fact function as title-deeds of the property. This is a sort of tit-for-tat, theft-for-theft.

4. Laban catches up with the caravan and throws the book at Jacob, with a whole lot of confused and contradictory ravings. Jacob has stolen the daughters away 'like prisoners of war', denying their father the chance of giving them an affectionate send-off. He has behaved like a fool. Laban has the power to harm him, but has been forbidden to do so by God. Anyway—and here is the nub—Jacob has stolen the title-deeds.

5. Jacob swears that he has stolen nothing. Laban (very sensibly!)

brushes the oath aside, but has enough delicacy to enable his own daughter to cheat him. It is a nice touch, and perhaps intentional, that, if Rachel's plea is true, she makes the 'household idols' unclean, for according to later legislation (Leviticus 15:20–23) anything a menstruating woman sits on becomes unclean.

6. With a fine show of righteous indignation Jacob pours out a list of the benefits he has conferred on the ungrateful Laban, and of his own personal heroism for Laban's sake. He repeats the charge of continual change of wages, and piously ascribes the outcome to God's judgment and special protection.

This is as ugly a row between in-laws as could be desired, narrated with great vivacity and verisimilitude: half-truths, unfounded accusations, deception, misrepresentation, bravado, exaggeration, personal challenges, lost tempers. The author of this burlesque must surely intend the audience to conclude that all the parties involved deserved everything they got.

The Kinsman of Isaac

The most obvious meaning of this title for God (in verse 42) is 'the Fear of Isaac', referring to Isaac's awe and reverence for his God. This would yield a moving trio of titles connected with the three patriarchs, characterizing the principal aspects under which God was revealed to them: 'the God of Abraham, the Fear of Isaac, the Mighty One of Jacob'. But this meaning for the Hebrew word is uncertain. Other strong suggestions have been 'Kinsman', stressing the family relationship and support of God for Isaac, and (relying on an Arabic word), 'the Refuge of Isaac'.

PRAYER

Lord God, you do not expect even your chosen representatives to be perfect, and you give us this example to inspire us in our own failures. I too can be less than honest, less than fair, even to those closest to me. Enable me to learn from this explosion how harmful this can all be, and keep me from it in the future.

37

GENESIS 31:43—32:3

A treaty between Jacob and Laban

Two pacts, two memorials

The text is heavily overloaded with agreements and their memorials. There seem to be two agreements, or at least two different subjects of agreement. The first is a personal, family agreement suggested by Laban to protect his daughters; this seems to show Laban, despite his threats, making the best of a bad job: he cannot get his daughters back, but at least he binds Jacob on oath not to set them aside or ill-treat them. The second agreement (verses 51–53a) is a territorial one, a non-aggression pact by which neither party is to pass a boundary mark.

These events are marked and commemorated by a double cairn-building and naming. There is a cairn of stones collected together. Laban calls this (in Aramaic) *Jegar-Sahadutha*, while Jacob gives it the same name in Hebrew (*Galeed*); both mean 'cairn of witness'. Aramaic is the wider language; originally the language of Syrian nomads, especially in Laban's area, it eventually became the international diplomatic and court language of the whole of the Near East, so that Hebrew almost went out of use, except as a sacred language. The Hebrew name is no doubt also related to the name of the wider district thereabouts, Gilead, the mountainous region which stands as a border between Israel and the desert. By this story it is marked out as the border between Laban's and Jacob's regions.

A second commemorative witness is provided by the pillar (in Hebrew *mazzebah*). There are a number of upright standing-stones of great antiquity in the region. It is also related to the name Mizpah, which means 'watchpost'. There will have been a settlement or town of that name in the region.

The duplication of pacts has a third element: besides these two physical memorials, two covenant meals seal and mark these two pacts (verses 46 and 54).

In short, all these memories and memorials testify to a peace finally made between the ancestors of Israel and those of the people of the deserts to the east. As often in these stories of the early folk-history, the history of the peoples is seen in that of their personal ancestors. On the whole this peace held, though there were times of incursions and invasions. In the time of the Judges the 'sons of the East' invaded repeatedly until they were repulsed by Gideon (Judges 6–8). Today also it is a border area, the eerily deserted Golan Heights between Israel and Syria, a sad memorial of later border strife.

The God of Abraham and the god of Nahor

A fascinating little possible remnant of polytheism, and of the difference between the two contracting parties, is provided by the oath formula, 'May the God of Abraham and the god of Nahor judge between us.' In the original languages the verb is plural, envisaging two gods, one of each party (in English singular and plural are indistinguishable in this state of the verb). God is still conceived as the personal protector of Abraham and his stock. 'The god of Nahor' is the personal protector of Nahor, Abraham's brother; this god is not necessarily considered to be the same deity, though it may be the same under a different name. How much did this religious difference enter into the strife within the family?

PRAYER

Lord, grant peace and justice between nations. Help all the nations of the world to realize that we are one family, and that in the last analysis the interests of one are the interests of all. Grant honesty and integrity in political life, and a real care for those whom politicians are supposed to serve.

38

Preparations for the meeting with Esau

Jacob's precautions

Jacob's nervousness is hardly surprising, after the way he had treated his elder brother some fourteen years before. First he had taken advantage of the impulsive young man's ravenous hunger to filch his inheritance from him. Then (another version of the same behaviour) he had carefully deceived his aged and helpless father to filch the blessing which was the property of the elder brother.

Esau had been unable to defend himself at the time of these two incidents, but it would hardly be surprising if he took the opportunity now. Jacob was very vulnerable with the large mass of flocks won by the further deception of his father-in-law. It looks as though his previous trickery is going to get its punishment at last, and presumably Esau himself has become powerful also in the interval.

Jacob's approach is to lay on a gradual build-up, one present after another, perhaps to increase the suspense, perhaps to suggest to Esau that there is no end to these presents. The series of incidents seems to be associated with the place called Mahanaim, meaning 'two camps'. The two camps enter into the story in various ways: in 32:8 Jacob divides the people into two camps so that one may be able to escape if Esau attacks the other. In 32:11 the two camps are an indication of Jacob's accumulation of wealth; the separation would be a necessity if large flocks and herds were to find grazing. In 33:8 the two camps represent an advance present for Esau before the main body.

The first exchange between Jacob and Esau is ominous. Jacob sends news of his considerable wealth, claiming that his motive is to win Esau's favour—perhaps by showing that he is an ally worth having, perhaps as a possible opening for bargaining. In the message he sends to Esau Jacob 'lays it on with a trowel', stressing the repeated phrases 'my lord' and 'your servant'. All this diplomacy seems to be brushed summarily aside. The succinct response on the return of the men sent by Jacob that Esau is on his way with 400 men obviously scares Jacob and suggests to him that a military posse is approaching. His reaction is triple: he divides into two camps, he falls to prayer, and he prepares the handsome gift for his brother.

Some hold that we have here two alternative traditions. The main narrative centres Jacob's preparation on the division into two camps and on the prayer. The warm and intimate language of the prayer is typical of the Yahwist (see Introduction), and especially its touching and thoughtful gratitude ('I had only my staff when I crossed this Jordan'). In fact the reference to the promises and to Yahweh's 'faithful love and constancy' is like a theme song which echoes down the scriptures. It is repeated more than once in this story itself.

In the later history of Israel this same appeal to God's promises and his faithfulness recurs whenever Israel gets into difficulties. In the New Testament similarly it becomes the message of the three canticles of Mary, Zechariah and Simeon in Luke's infancy stories: 'Now, Lord, let your servant depart in peace, according to your word, for my eyes have seen the salvation which you have prepared in the sight of every nation.' In the Pauline writings, from Romans to Ephesians, the fulfilment of God's promises in Christ is the central theme.

The preparation of the very handsome gift (32:14b–22) would then be the Elohistic version (see Introduction). There was no reason why Esau should be particularly hostile here, for in 28:1–8 Jacob had merely gone off on Isaac's instructions to find a wife. There was no story of deception or taking advantage. The two sets of preparation may well be independent. It is certainly a little odd that there is no reference to the elaborate and generous courtesy of the gifts when they actually meet.

PRAYER

Lord, help me to be honest in my dealings with others and with you. Give me the confidence to face facts as they are, knowing that I have your promises to rely on, however grim a situation looks.

39
Jacob wrestles with God

This haunting narrative intrigues by its many layers and facets. At a superficial level it is a mass of explanations of names and custom. The River Jabbok flows into the Jordan just below the Lake of Galilee, forming a magnificent break in the eastern hills from which Jacob is coming after leaving Laban. There is a pun on this name: 'wrestles' uses the root *'abaq*.

Explanations of the place name Peniel and of the tribal name Israel are also offered, and of the tabu on eating the sinew of the hip socket (not mentioned elsewhere in the Bible). One puzzle is why Jacob should attempt to cross the river at all (let alone in the middle of the night, with his people and his flocks); the river does not lie on his route, and he is next seen again, as before, on the north side of it.

In its context of the meeting with Esau, the story seems to be a response to Jacob's prayer: after his prayer and before the actual meeting Jacob receives a renewal of the blessing, and also the new name. The gift of a name always represents not only a new nature or a new status but also a taking possession by the giver of the name. The meaning of the name 'Israel' is more likely 'May God rule/show his strength', but here it is related to *sarah el*, 'struggle against God'.

The underlying story, however, is more mysterious. It seems to be based on some primitive magical encounter with a river-sprite who rules the crossing-point of this fierce torrent (I have seen it only in summer, and even then it boils and roars turbulently) and wishes to prevent passage. The story itself wavers over the divinity of the opponent, initially calling him 'a man' but finally granting that Jacob has 'seen God face to face'. The mysterious creature, a sort of night-spirit, must disappear with the dawn. To give Jacob its name would give Jacob some power over it, so it refuses to divulge its name.

There is a contrast here with Yahweh's gift of a name to Moses at the Burning Bush, a sign of Yahweh's intimacy with and friendship for Moses. On the other hand, there is a strange similarity between this story and the eerie story of Exodus 4:24, when Yahweh tries to kill Moses and ends up by circumcising him. Both must be reflections of primitive fears of the unknown.

Who comes off best at Peniel? Jacob is wounded, but will not let go. Jacob does acknowledge the superiority of his opponent by asking a blessing, but the blessing is interpreted 'you have shown your strength against God and men and have prevailed'. In another version of the story, which may well be more primitive (Hosea 12:3–5), Jacob is blamed as much for this incident as for his supplanting his brother: 'He wrestled with the angel and beat him, he wept and pleaded with him.'

Whatever the origins of this story, its meaning and function in the narrative as it stands do seem to be significant. It seems like a conversion story; God takes final possession of Jacob in this mysterious encounter. Hereafter we hear no more of Jacob's trickery and dishonesty. Whatever exactly went on, by this experience of the divine or supernatural being he is, so to speak, made an honest patriarch and at last settles down to be a model cornerstone of his people.

PRAYER

Lord God, you work in mysterious ways, and it is often difficult for us to see the true significance of events, to understand how your hand is guiding us. Often, too, an experience seems too hurtful at the time, and only later can we understand that we are being touched by your healing hand.

40 The meeting with Esau

The meeting

Despite all the nervousness shown by Jacob in his preparations, when the brothers actually meet Esau is magnanimous enough to brush aside all Jacob's offerings and simply welcome him as a brother. The contrast between the two is amusingly painted: Jacob's nervousness is shown by his distribution of his wives and children. The least precious of his wives (and their children) are put nearest the approaching and possibly hostile troops, while the beloved Rachel (and her son) is kept at the back, furthest from danger.

Jacob himself remains formal, bowing seven times to the ground, and insisting on calling his brother 'my lord'. Despite Esau's unwillingness Jacob insists that he accept the series of presents. He had already said (32:9) that he regarded the front 'camp' as expendable: if Esau turned out to be hostile, he could keep those while the others made their escape.

On Jacob's part there is a great deal of oriental courtesy and formality in the meeting. One feels that there must be some motive behind this insistence, over and above brotherly affection. It would be perfectly natural that Esau's acceptance of the gift would bind him not to molest Jacob, while if he refuses he will still be able to hold himself free to do his brother harm. This would explain why Jacob is so keen to get the gift accepted.

By contrast to his obsequious brother, Esau, the rough man of the desert, is a great deal more cheerful and natural, replying to the elaborate ceremonial of seven bows to the ground with the heartiest and least formal of hugs. He really is not interested in the gifts— 'Brother, I have plenty'—and remains the same generous and devil-may-care open-hearted fellow that he was when he bartered away his birthright for a square meal. This is a splendid little bit of characterization, which is unusual in the Bible (character-drawing is not usual in any ancient literature; it does not seem to have interested writers and readers at the time).

Nevertheless, the cautious and calculating Jacob is determined not to prolong their meeting, and, after Esau's display of affection, hustles him off ahead on the excuse that his own party cannot stand the pace—presumably after their previous long marches. Jacob's camp, since it is the whole clan on the move, also includes the vulnerable young, both human and animal, whom Esau will have been able to leave at home.

Esau moves off to Seir, the mountainous desert of the south-east, and disappears temporarily from the story. The elaborate meeting seems to have no further consequences, and simply fizzles out. Jacob settles for the moment at Succoth, which means 'shelters'. As usual, there is a pun on the name. The town is traditionally located on the east side of the Jordan Valley. Soon Jacob will go up to the hill-country, which would become the traditional home of the Israelites descended from him.

PRAYER

Lord, grant me sensitivity to those whom I meet, an awareness of their needs and desires. Save me from blundering in with my own preoccupations, but make me always alert and open to the other person.

41 The rape of Dinah

The first three verses give a dry and factual account of Jacob's settlement in Shechem. He simply buys the land and dedicates it by erecting an altar, as had Abraham at Bethel and Hebron. The story of the rape of Dinah which follows gives a more circumstantial account, not without its difficulties.

A composite narrative

The story presupposes a new situation. It does not follow on from the previous stories, where Jacob's children are still young; here they are all fully grown. It describes the attempt at settlement in Canaan. The basic facts are that the person Shechem and his father Hamor both stand for the town of Shechem. A primitive feature which attaches the story to early times is that circumcision does not yet appear to have any connection with the covenant, as it does in all later, Deuteronomic, theology; it is only a distinguishing mark of the clan, not the sign of commitment to Yahweh.

In view of this story it is remarkable that in the account of the conquest of Canaan by Joshua no account is given of the appropriation of this geographically important town. This is all the more notable in that the final chapter of the book (Joshua 24) locates at Shechem a great unifying assembly, at which all the people commit themselves again to the covenant. This must be an expression of a renewal of the covenant to include all those who had joined Israel since the departure from Egypt. It is commemorated by a stone, no doubt the same monument as is mentioned here in 33:20 as set up by Jacob. The story of Jesus and the woman at the well of Jacob in John 4 is a further reminder that the town became Jacob's centre, for 'Sychar', the location of that well, is the Aramaic form of Shechem.

The complications of the narrative are considerable: sometimes Shechem and sometimes his father Hamor conduct the negotiations. Sometimes the rape of Dinah is at issue, sometimes it does not seem to feature at all. The easiest solution to these puzzles is to grant that the story moves on two levels. Both relate the settlement of Jacob's clan at Shechem: one moves by means of a story concerning individuals (Simeon and Levi, Shechem and Dinah), the other covers the same ground on a more generalized level. It is impressive that on both levels the memory has been preserved of unjustifiable treachery on the part of Israel's ancestors. The clarity of the two levels was later obscured by some attempts to link the two together.

1. A personal level: Shechem rapes and fall in love with Dinah (verses 1–5). He then tries desperately to win her in marriage, offering whatever bride-price her family desire (verses 11–12). The family reply that any husband must be circumcised (verse 14), and Shechem willingly accepts this condition (verse 19). Two brothers of Dinah, Simeon and Levi, treacherously renege on their agreement, take advantage of Shechem and his household when they are still incapacitated by their wounds, and withdraw Dinah (verses 25–26).

2. A tribal level, concerning the settlement of Jacob's clan in the town. Hamor's speech to Jacob's sons (verses 8–10) concerns general intermarriage, not simply an individual couple, so that the whole clan can acquire holdings and have the freedom of the country. Their reply in verses 15–16 also concerns the whole groups, circumcision of all the males, so that 'we will give you our daughters'. The agreement is then ratified by the elders of the town in session at the city-gate (verses 20–24). Finally there is a general pillage not just of one family but of the whole town and seizure of flocks in a general raid by Jacob's sons (verses 27–29).

Later touches are provided by such verses as verse 7. Since the brothers say that Shechem has insulted Israel, this presupposes that the nation already exists as a recognizable entity. Their following comment about the unacceptability of the conduct occurs also as an integral part of the story of another rape, that of Tamar by Amnon in 2 Samuel 13:12; it gives a strong impression of fitting originally there.

PRAYER

Lord, even your chosen people broke their agreements and used violence against the innocent. Now that you have educated us for so long, and especially have given us the example of your Son Jesus Christ, grant us to shun violence and injustice. Grant peace and tolerance, even appreciation, among the peoples of your world.

GENESIS 35:1-20
Jacob at Bethel

The pilgrimage to Bethel

This is really the final chapter of the Jacob cycle, gathering together oddments of the tradition, of which the largest and most continuous piece concerns the move to Bethel. It seems unlikely that Jacob had any permanent residence, or any permanent centre apart from the family burial plot at Hebron, bought by Abraham. He appears to range freely over several places, that is, there were several sanctuaries which had associations with his name.

We have already had one story of Jacob's sacred association with Bethel, the story of Jacob's Ladder. The present story may be a mere alternative, reflecting a special sort of pilgrimage cult. It starts with a purification, getting rid of the foreign gods. This may envisage the 'household gods' brought as title-deeds from Laban's property, but it is no doubt wider than this. The earrings were presumably cult objects too. Crescent-shaped gold earrings of the period have been found in quantity in buried hoards in Israel: they would be relics of the worship of the moon which was common in those parts, and especially in the homeland of Abraham's clan. So these ancestral earrings will have been relics also of ancestral religion, which must be removed.

A change of clothes is also often the sign of a new beginning, and frequently specifically of a sacred action. On Sinai, in preparation for the covenant, the people are told to wash their clothes as part of sanctifying themselves (Exodus 19:10–11), and the priests put on special clothes for their function. These are natural signs; we all understand the significance of freshening up and dressing up for a party.

The picture is completed by verse 5, which should really be the conclusion of the incident at Shechem: the 'divine terror' explains why no one pursued the sons of Jacob after their devastating raid on the town. The close link of this verse to that incident suggests not so much that this verse has been displaced as that the other preparations have been inserted before the original conclusion. Now the 'divine terror' is a sort of awe which accompanies the pilgrimage.

The promise to Israel

This is a solemn moment in the history of the chosen people. After all his wanderings and somewhat dubious activities, Jacob has arrived in the land and has begun to settle. At this stage some reassurance of the special vocation of his clan is needed. He dedicates anew himself and the land by building an altar—'and all the people with him' (verse 6). God indicates acceptance of this homage by appearing to Jacob, and then takes the significant step of giving him a new name, the name which will be that of the people of Israel.

It matters not that Jacob has already received this name and its explanation at the River Jabbok, for that narrative belongs to a different source. God then repeats the command to be fruitful and multiply which had been so often addressed to Abraham. It is as a memorial of this solemn promise that Jacob sets up the standing-stone at Bethel, which may be the heart of the story.

Two deaths

It is curious that the death of Rebekah's nurse should be recorded at this point; it is presumably a topographical note, explaining the Oak of Tears which was known at Bethel. Most likely also the tomb of Rachel, which explains the insertion here of the sad note on Rachel's death, was situated near Bethel. This is suggested by verse 16, which would make nonsense of the identification with Bethlehem, given in verse 19.

[There is no commentary on 35:21—36:43, which simply consists of records in the Priestly tradition.]

PRAYER

Lord God, every now and then I need the reassurance of your love for me. I have committed myself to you, and know that you are always there and attentive to my needs. But give me these signs of your care and open my eyes to see them.

43 Joseph sold into slavery

The Joseph story

Chapters 37–46 (with the exception of 38) form a single, coherent whole, unlike anything else in Genesis. They are united round the person of Joseph and round two themes, the quarrel and reconciliation within the circle of brothers, and the rise of Joseph to power in Egypt. In its present form the story has been judged to date from the reign of Solomon. At this period there was in Israel considerable cultural interest in Egypt, as Solomon borrowed various features from Egypt in developing his own monarchy; and yet the knowledge displayed is neither so complete nor so accurate as to suggest inside experience. In addition the story of Joseph's rise to power in Egypt reflects certain features well known from Egyptian literature.

This does not mean that the Joseph story is a work of fiction without foundation in fact. Some historical nucleus is needed to explain the transfer of Jacob's family to Egypt and their position in the land. But the remembered historical nucleus has been developed into the present memorable gem of a story.

Joseph and his brothers

The beginning of the Joseph story revolves round dissension within the family; this will be the underlying theme until it is finally resolved by Joseph's settlement of the family within his territory. This first incident crystallizes round the long-sleeved coat, first the sign of the father's infuriating indulgence of the cocky, upstart son of his old age, and then the triumphant (even if untrue) evidence that the brothers have taken their revenge on the upstart and on their father's favouritism. Only its familiarity can blind us to the dramatic tension and suspense of the story.

It seems that two sources have been combined in the central incident of the story. In one (verses 18–25a, 28a, 29–30) Reuben is the leader of the brothers, anxious to avoid hurting his father; Joseph is simply dumped in a well, to cool off while the brothers have a hearty meal. From there he is kidnapped by some passing Midianites—to the horrified surprise of Reuben, when he finds the well empty. In the other source (verses 25b–27, 28b) Judah leads the planning, and Joseph is sold to Ishmaelites, as a way of getting rid of him without the brothers actually shedding his blood.

The characterization of the participants is brilliant. The pert little favourite starts both accounts of his self-congratulatory dreams (dreams are, of course, a feature of the Joseph story) with a command to his elders, 'Listen!...', 'Look!...' Even the indulgent father is given pause for thought and 'pondered the matter'. It needs no Jung to discern the thoughtless complacency expressing itself insistently in both dreams. By contrast, after a tremulous farewell from his old father (he twice wishes '*Shalom!*', peace), the young fellow is so upset that he is found helplessly wandering around in the countryside.

The two elder brothers of the group are nicely distinguished. Reuben tries to restrain the brothers and keep them to mere bullying. He is distraught at the disappearance of the boy. Judah, by contrast, is more brutal. He eggs the brothers on, and himself proposes the sale, wanting to be as unpleasant as possible while still saving their own skin from blood-guilt.

The story is a perfect example of God protecting the weak, and of drawing good out of evil. When it comes to the point, the lost and incapable child is totally helpless before the gang of his ten elder brothers ('We saw his deep misery when he pleaded with us', they admit many years later: 42:21). What a welcome, when he eventually sights them after his miserable wanderings! Not only does all this lead eventually to Joseph's own preferment, but if Joseph had not had his position in Egypt, the tribe of Jacob would never have won their favoured position there.

PRAYER

Lord God, we sometimes feel as lost as Joseph, and wonder whether even you, the Father of our family, have deserted us and thrown us into the pit. Give me the confidence to trust that, even when my situation is desperate, you are at my side.

44

The story of Judah and Tamar

This nicely turned story interrupts the story of Joseph. It concerns another of Jacob's sons, the eldest and the ancestor of the largest and most important tribe, Judah. The link with the previous story is provided by Judah's leading role in the sale of his young brother into Egypt, but the stories are quite unconnected. The story of Judah is much older and not only the age but also the character of Judah quite different. The age of the story is shown by several features: Judah is quite at ease among the Canaanites. There is no worry about Judah taking a Canaanite wife, which must have preceded the Priestly concern for purity of the stock (as shown in the trouble taken by Abraham and Isaac to obtain wives for their sons from their own stock, and the disdain for Esau's 'Hittite' wives).

The law of the levirate

Another ancient feature is the crux of the story: the levirate law. If a married man dies without issue to carry on his name, his nearest male relative is obliged to father a child for the widow, who counts as the heir of the dead man and carries on his line. (In later legislation the nearest male relative is obliged to *marry* the widow; this is the situation envisaged by the Sadducees' trick question to Jesus in Mark 12:9). In this story Onan's sin is not any sexual perversion, but that he avoids carrying out this duty, while presumably giving the family the impression that he is fulfilling it.

On her husband's death the widow reverts to the custody of her father-in-law, whose duty it is to see that the line is carried on. Judah, however, having failed with two of his sons, first fobs the widow off with a promise of future marriage with someone who is still too young, and then lets her down by giving this son to another. The widow is therefore left to her own resources, and Judah, besides being her guardian, is her nearest male relative! It is his duty to ensure her a son.

The wit of the story lies in several features. The first is the bawdy amusement of the hearer at the reprehensible behaviour of the venerable patriarch, ancestor of this great clan. As soon as he gets away on holiday—he and his crony, Hirah—from territory where he is known, he heads for the red-light district. As he has been improvident enough not to bring cash, he has to hand over the ancient equivalents of his car keys and credit card (the seal and the carved staff serve the function of personal identity-markers in the Mesopotamian world—myriads of different carefully made pottery cylindrical seals have been found).

Further discomfiture follows when he fails to recover these precious tokens. She who laughs last, laughs longest, and in this case, after a cliffhanger finale, it is Tamar. Perhaps most interesting is the quiet dignity with which Judah accepts that Tamar has outwitted him and made him do his duty—the first of many cases in the Bible (like Luke's unjust judge) of someone doing the right thing from the wrong motive.

Step by step

In spite of what was said earlier (in commenting on the Garden of Eden) about the equality of the sexes in Israel, there is a crying inequality in the legislation on sexual misconduct. She is to be burnt, he not even censured for his one-night stand, though he does himself admit that he was in the wrong. Doomed is any attempt to claim that even the moral principles in Israel, let alone the practice, were perfect from the start. Education in moral matters, as in the knowledge of God, was and is a gradual process. The slaughter of prisoners of war was considered an act of homage to God. But then even Christians vigorously supported the slave trade. There may be issues on which God has still to refine our moral sensibility today.

PRAYER

Lord God, the sexual union between man and woman which you instituted is a lovely thing, and the nobility of joining in your act of creation is a great human dignity. But the process certainly is fraught with dangers and temptations. Grant that I may esteem the nobility of sex so highly that I hold myself clear of its misuse and its distortions.

45

Joseph's early days in Egypt

The next two stories deal with Joseph's rise to power in Egypt, again by God's help bringing good out of evil. As the names used for God make clear, the first is from the Yahwistic tradition (with its lively characterization and vigorous action), the second from the Elohistic tradition (with its emphasis on dreams). From the beginning of Joseph's career in Egypt the reader is impressed by his uprightness and fidelity to the Lord in all that he does. Throughout the stories it is frequently stressed that 'Yahweh was with Joseph and everything he undertook was successful'. In this incident one typical detail of his fidelity to his religion is that Potiphar has entrusted to him everything except the matter of food; this may be an allusion to Joseph's care for food restrictions in accordance with the Law—though it may also mean that Joseph is so efficient that Potiphar has nothing left to do but make a pig of himself!

The seductress

The story of the attempted seduction of Joseph has a classic pattern. There was a similar well-known Egyptian story of two brothers, in which the wife of the elder brother tried to induce the younger brother to sleep with her while her husband was out in the fields.

The later Wisdom books of the Bible (where the Egyptian influence is strong) constantly warn against the seductress—an interesting contrast to modern society, in which the classic pattern of such stories is the company director seducing his female secretary, or the doctor his female patient.

Perhaps in a society so male-dominated as that of the ancient East, a man taking advantage of a woman earned no comment. Either way, perhaps more otherwise fruitful and blameless careers are ruined by failure in this area than in any other. Hence Joseph's resolute self-control is a warrant of his firmness and reliability in other spheres.

He knows that he is in a wretched position, with no rights and on a hiding to nothing whatever he does. The mistress's word is bound to prevail against the slave, and the only course of action open to her to protect her own skin is to accuse the handsome young man. But still Joseph endangers himself for the sake of his integrity.

Another aspect of his action—and always an important facet of such eternal triangles—is Joseph's loyalty to his master, her husband. It is the human relationship rather than the physical act which is most important, for the human relationship always suffers most, snarled up in a web of deception, mistrust and suspicion.

Joseph's progress continues

Joseph's imprisonment provides a useful link to the story which follows. Even in prison Yahweh does not abandon his faithful love for Joseph. So Joseph bobs to the top again—a feature not required by the link to the next story.

PRAYER

You are my hope, Lord,
my trust, Yahweh, since boyhood.
On you have I relied since my birth,
since my mother's womb you have been my portion.
Psalm 71

46

Joseph interprets dreams in prison

Joseph has to undergo one more test before his trials are over. This adds to the long list of frustrations: sale by his brothers (or kidnapping), slavery, false accusation and imprisonment. Now he again shows the special favour he receives from God and his special closeness to God and reliance upon him, only to find again how little reliance can be placed on human beings. His interpretation of the dreams is correct, but the chief cup bearer is so delighted at his release that he forgets all about Joseph and leaves him languishing in the jail.

Dreams

So far in Genesis, and generally in the older part of the Old Testament, dreams have been a way of communication from God, a sort of meeting with God. In Genesis they are a characteristic of the Elohistic narratives. Thus God appears in a dream to Abimelech and warns him not to touch Sarah (Genesis 20:3), and to Laban to warn him not to harm Jacob (Genesis 31:2).

Jacob himself is given instructions in a dream how to acquire a vigorous flock (Genesis 31:10). Especially dreams are a way in which God assures his chosen friends of his protection: Hagar (Genesis 21:17), Isaac (Genesis 26:24), and, most of all, Jacob's ladder (Genesis 28:12). The same is true of the rare dreams later in the earlier part of the Bible: Solomon receives the promise of the gift of wisdom in a dream in the sanctuary at Gibeon (1 Kings 3:5–15).

In modern religious experience the same is also true. Psychoanalysis has shown that dreams often reveal the deep emotions and repressions which we cannot face in waking hours, and so enable us to reach a new understanding of ourselves. This may itself be a gift from God, and the occasion of a new or deeper understanding of his will. It is clearly a time at which we are most sensitive and receptive to ideas which we do not normally entertain. It is therefore not surprising that dreams often seem to be the occasion when God communicates directly with human beings.

The dreams in the Joseph story, however, are different. They reflect a much more magical and superstitious approach to dreams, in which the dreams are simply a coded prediction of the future, without any divine content. This conception was widespread in Egypt, and generally in the ancient Near East. Books of interpretation existed, and the business was considered an expert science. According to an Egyptian book of this period, to see a large cat meant a good harvest, to see the moon meant forgiveness from the gods, looking into a deep well meant imprisonment.

The dream in some sense symbolically mirrors the future event. This is the pattern of the two dreams of the royal officials in this chapter. But the attitude of the Joseph story (and later of the Book of Daniel) is a critique of this quasi-scientific approach to dreams: they are the gift of God and can be interpreted only with his help. But still, the Egyptian atmosphere is still retained, in that the only connection with God is that the information is sent by God, and that his chosen messenger can decode the dream. They do not bring the dreamer closer to God, nor reveal anything of the divine nature.

Joseph the sage

In this story for the first time we see Joseph, as the interpreter of dreams, fulfilling the ideal of the wise man who receives his wisdom from God. The Wisdom tradition (enshrined in the Wisdom books of the Bible) came to Israel largely from Egypt. Many of the principles and counsels of this tradition are concerned with good sense, court behaviour, how to get on in the world, practical ability, as well as the more profound ways of wisdom. In the case of Joseph and his advancement, then, this is part of the local colouring of the story.

PRAYER

Lord God, forgetfulness of past benefits is one of the hazards of life. Grant me to remember those to whom I have a debt of gratitude. Save me also from disappointment and resentment when my own efforts are forgotten.

47 Pharaoh's dream

At last we come to the turning-point in Joseph's fortunes, after his two years languishing in prison. At every stage it is stressed that reversal of fortune and blessing come directly from God, without whom nothing can succeed. Joseph stresses (four times) that skill in interpretation comes from Yahweh, not from himself. His rise to power is as well deserved as it is inevitable. ·

The story is again beautifully told. To mention only a few delightful narrative touches: one can almost feel the frantic rush to get the dishevelled and neglected Joseph shaved and spruced up to be presentable to Pharaoh. Next, Joseph's dignity before Pharaoh as he stands his ground and corrects him, 'Not I. God will give Pharaoh a favourable answer', and then waits silently for Pharaoh to begin.

The dreams form a neat pair, as did the prisoners' dreams in the previous chapter. Pharaoh's panic makes him quite excited and dramatic as he tells the dreams: in the original dream the cows were 'wretched and lean'; in his recounting they become '*starved, very* wretched and lean; *I have never seen such poor cows in all Egypt*'. He also adds that it was impossible to tell that the lean cows had eaten the fat ones. The ears of grain were 'withered and scorched'; in his version they become 'withered, *meagre* and scorched'.

When Joseph has finished the interpretation, he silently leaves the next move to Pharaoh, not pushing himself forward or offering himself for the job. There is no sign of self-congratulation at all the splendour which is thrust upon him; he quietly gets on with the task in hand.

The local colour is all authentic. In his dream Pharaoh is standing beside the Nile; this is fitting, for the annual flooding of the Nile brings down the silt which makes the land fertile. The investiture follows procedures we know from documents: as King Assurbanipal of Assyria invests Pharaoh Necho as his vice-regent he says (on the inscribed Rassam Cylinder, found in 1878), 'I clad him in a garment with multicoloured trimmings, placed a gold chain on him as the insignia of his kingship, put golden rings on his hands. I presented him with chariots, mules and horses.' All these symbols are familiar also from Egyptian tomb-paintings. Only 'Abrek!', the cry of homage as he is driven around in his Daimler, has foxed all interpreters.

The Egyptian names do not quite fit the period, having a form common in Egypt two centuries later. Joseph's name means 'God speaks; he lives.' His wife's name means 'belonging to the goddess Neith', and her father's temple at On is a famous sanctuary of the sun-god. Joseph's tour of inspection suggests that Pharaoh owned all the agricultural land in Egypt (see 47:20), and the vast granaries are often mentioned in Egyptian records. The intricate bureaucracy presupposed for the collection and distribution certainly existed in that highly sophisticated civilization.

Joseph's sons

A sequence familiar from the earlier patriarchal stories, quite unlike the Egyptian material, follows with the etymology of the names of Joseph's sons. As usual, it is somewhat forced: Manasseh is linked to the Hebrew *nahshani*=he has made me forget, and Ephraim to *hiphrani*=he has made me fruitful.

PRAYER
Lord, give me the dignity like Joseph to accept disaster without despair and success without vanity. Make me always remember that achievement comes from your guiding hand and your blessing.

48 The first meeting of Joseph and his brothers

With this meeting the story begins to turn to the final resolution. The historical background is perfectly normal. Just as Abraham went down to Egypt in time of drought and famine, so do modern nomads. Fragmentary contemporary reports of officials at the carefully controlled frontier have been found, for instance: 'We have finished letting the shepherd tribes of Edom pass the fortress of Merneptah, to keep them alive and to keep their cattle alive.' In Roman times Egypt was the bread basket of the Mediterranean where food was sure to be found.

The irony of the situation

The account is full of reminiscences of the earlier family scenes. This brings dramatic irony into ample play: the reader, knowing so much more than the brothers, sees far more significance in their words and situation. This is made all the more intriguing by the useful props, the one-sided recognition by Joseph, combined with their failure to recognize this finely clad viceroy, and Joseph's ability to listen in, unnoticed, to their conversation.

The brothers are straitjacketed by Jacob's fear that something may happen to Benjamin as it did to the other son of his old age. They still have a deep underlying sense of guilt, prompted, perhaps, by the memory that the Ishmaelite purchasers were on their way to Egypt. When his brothers bow down before him, Joseph is reminded of that fatal dream which caused all the trouble. Most important of all, Joseph's inflexibility is seen by them as God's own punishment for their old cruelty to him. Now at last is their crime brought home to them.

It must be admitted, however, that the less pleasant side of Joseph's character now comes to the fore. The biblical author suggests that Joseph is unkind to them as he 'remembers the dreams he had about them', and plays with them as cat with mouse. He has no hesitation in hitting the ten men who are down, repeating insistently that they are spies. The half-starved, guilt-ridden suppliants can offer only the feeble circumstantial reasoning that spies are single, hard men, not a large family group (families with children are never suspected as hijackers or terrorists). Without compunction—perhaps even as deliberate revenge for his own sojourn in the cistern—he claps them in the cooler for three days.

Then the author dwells on Joseph's awareness of their misery as they watch Simeon being bound as the hostage. Only a couple of little human touches shine through, when Joseph shows consideration for their starving families back home, and when he sheds a tear at the discovery, after all these years, that at least Reuben had tried to protect him against the callousness of the others.

Two accounts?

Strong arguments have been put forward that the author has combined two accounts. Joseph really does insist too many times that they are spies. He seems to have two different plans, first demanding that one of the brothers bring Benjamin while all the others remain as hostages, then keeping only Simeon as hostage. Similarly, in the following account of the return journey, they find the money in their sacks or saddle bags (the Hebrew consistently uses two different words) twice, each time being equally surprised. This is hardly plausible psychologically, but is defensible from a literary point of view.

PRAYER

Lord, so much can go wrong in a family, and especially with the pressures of modern living and working. You made us different personalities, even within a family, and this provides richness and variety. Grant that I may admire the differences and talents of my family, and love them all the more for not being me!

Jacob's sons return for Benjamin

The tension is now mounting towards some sort of dénouement. We seem to be in an impasse: no chance of food or the release of the hostage Simeon unless Benjamin is brought to Egypt. No chance of Jacob allowing Benjamin to go. Every touch reminds the brothers of their guilt of long ago.

Two accounts

Here the duplication of the accounts really emerges: in verses 27–28 on the first evening of the journey one of the brothers finds his money returned to him in the mouth of his donkey-feed bag; in verse 35 they all find the money at home when they are unpacking after delivering their report to Jacob. For the author who combined them, however, these two occasions serve different purposes: the first fills them with awe at the mysterious workings of God ('What is this that God has done to us?'); so struck with remorse for their crime are they by now, that they see the disaster as the work of God, nothing to do with human agency. The second occasion provokes only fear, and serves as a reminder to Jacob about the loss of his sons, setting his self-pity really going. The discovery of the money destroys their last chance of persuading him! The irony is that the Joseph they had sold for money now returns to them the same money!

Family tensions

Another amusing feature is the little expansions and twists which the brothers give to the story in negotiation with their father. They claim that if they take Benjamin they will obtain not only the release of Simeon but the right to move freely about the country (verse 34), which Joseph had never suggested. They avoid upsetting Jacob by deliberately passing over the three days they had spent in the cooler. As the hunger bites more and more urgently, they fib that Joseph threatened to refuse even an audience unless they brought Benjamin. When Jacob reproaches them for telling 'the Egyptian' about the family, they make up a whole rigmarole of detailed interrogation.

The great skill of the story-teller is that he makes sure that the characters remain the same as they were in the story of the abduction of Joseph. Jacob is crotchety and full of self-pity. He is still calling the shots, and (typical old man) insists on treating Benjamin as a child. On any calculation Benjamin must be a young adult by now, though he is always referred to in the subsequent discussions as 'the boy'. Jacob can think only of his own loss: 'I bear the brunt of all this.' (Nevertheless, he still manages to speak in nicely balanced rhythm: 1. 'You are robbing me of my children.' 2. 'Joseph is no more.' 2. 'Simeon is no more.' 1. 'Now you want to take Benjamin.')

Reuben, who had tried to protect Joseph, is again the generous one, and offers his own children as hostages to fortune. He asks for Benjamin to be put in his care, insinuating that he is more caring and trustworthy than the others. By contrast, the rough Judah, who had proposed the sale of Joseph, gives Jacob the ultimatum which finally tips the scales: 'If you are not prepared to send him, we will not go down.' Finally he takes the leadership and gets impatient with the whole discussion: 'let us be off and go,' he interrupts.

Finally convinced, the fussy old man gives his fully-grown sons, fathers themselves, detailed instructions about presents to 'the man' (whose name he refuses to pronounce). Yet somehow or other he gives the first hint of the dénouement with his hope that God may produce the missing brother too.

PRAYER

Lord, give me always the insight to see when I have wronged people. Jolt me to do your will, and especially to right the injustices I have committed.

50 The second journey to Egypt

The final resolution of the alienation of Joseph is painted with great artistry and human drama, but with clear realization that God is the architect of the reconciliation. Four scenes stand out: the mysterious reception by Joseph, the stolen cup, the intervention of Judah and the final reconciliation.

The mysterious reception (43:16–34)

The puzzlement which pervades this scene heightens the tension. Joseph is again playing cat-and-mouse. The brothers are tense and jumpy throughout, rightly suspicious of being taken to Joseph's own house, of the warmth of the chamberlain's reception, the sudden obliteration of their 'crime' of theft. The accusation is simply dropped, and Simeon merrily released. The chamberlain tells them to set their minds at ease and even uses the familiar formula 'Your God and the God of your fathers'.

Joseph keeps up his defences as well as he can. However, the symbol of his determination to keep his distance is the fact that he continues to eat apart as an Egyptian. And yet there is a new familiarity and warmth about him which the brothers find strange and eerie, as he asks about the family. The brothers relax no wit; they wisely keep up their prostrations and their obsequious self-entitlement, 'your servants'. They are amazed that he knows enough to place them correctly in order of seniority, but paradoxically gives the generous portion of honour to the youngest, Benjamin. He must have had a young man's appetite to cope with five times the normal portion!

This mysterious reserve right up to the final recognition scene makes that resolution of the discord all the more welcome and fitting.

The stolen cup (44:1–17)

This puzzling little incident must be intended to increase the tension still further, and to delay the resolution one last time. It seems quite unnecessary, a mere tantalizing device of Joseph's determination to torture his brothers. It oddly duplicates the previous incident of the money in the feed bags. The crime is, of course, much worse, since the cup is not only a personal possession but is put forward as a religious object. The fact that it is a repetition of the previous 'crime' makes it all the more horrific, since it calls in question the innocence which has just been so openly granted to them. Hence the vehement protestations of the brothers, and their extreme offers of self-sacrifice to prove their innocence.

Divination with a cup was one of many 'sciences' of discovering the future. References to practices of divination are scattered throughout the ancient Near Eastern religious texts. Some of them have survived: signs of good and bad luck, palm-reading, interpretation of dreams and other omens. The principal method with a cup was by interpreting the patterns of oil on the surface of water. The idea of Joseph practising such superstition is oddly at variance with the way he earlier stood apart from the professional interpreters of dreams, and with the later prohibition of divination on penalty of death. Presumably it was a lie, part of his deliberate campaign to tantalize the brothers one last time.

In any case, we end this incident in a worse situation than ever before, with the threat of the ultimate disaster: the loss of Benjamin. There is only one glimmer of hope: the brothers acknowledge their guilt (possibly with regard to young Joseph, possibly merely in general) and are beginning to show the generosity of sacrificing themselves for the family.

PRAYER

Lord God, protect me from slander and false accusation, and especially accusations and criticisms made behind my back. Grant me also to be straightforward in criticism when it must be made, honest and caring to those who are at fault.

51

The reconciliation
with Joseph

Judah intervenes (44:18–34)

This has been called one of the great speeches of the Old Testament. Gone is Judah's impatience and bluster. In the course of the dozen verses he twelve times uses the subservient 'your servant'. One is reminded of the Egyptian texts themselves, where every mention of the Pharaoh's name has to be followed by the repeated blessing, 'life, prosperity, health!' But the salient feature of the speech is the worried affection for the family and particularly for Jacob.

Jacob, rather than Benjamin, holds the chief attention at every point of this detailed rehearsal of the process of events. At all costs, whether this Egyptian is interested in the story or not, Jacob must be protected. It is notable that no mention is made of Joseph's strange behaviour, and no blame attached to him.

This conversion is surely important for the moral message of the story. The story of Joseph began with family enmity and rivalry. Particularly Judah was a leader in this, actually suggesting the callousness of selling the upstart young Joseph. Now, before the final resolution, he has shown another side of his character. Finally he offers himself insistently as a vicarious victim, 'I implore you' (verse 33).

The offering by the brothers after the discovery of the 'stolen' cup, and this individual offering by Judah, are the first acts of voluntary self-offering in the Bible. Isaac was to be offered in sacrifice by his father, but Judah puts himself forward.

This precious tradition will continue and develop in the self-offering of the Servant of the Lord in Isaiah, offering himself for the sins of others. It will reach its completion in Jesus' own sacrifice on the cross, and be carried on in the martyrs of the New Testament.

The reconciliation (45:1–15)

At last comes the revelation, with great intimacy and warmth. For the third time Joseph cannot restrain his tears. The dismissal of the servants makes it a totally family event, as in all affection he calls the brothers closer to him. It is also touching that his first question is about his father, and that he asks them to bring down his father quickly. The brothers are rightly dumbfounded after all his trickery, and it is only when he has kissed them all (Benjamin having a special place) that they recover and are sufficiently reassured to talk to him.

The theological clue to the whole chain of events of the Joseph story now appears in the triple repetition that this is all the work of God, in the divine design to bring the family down to Egypt. Joseph has become 'father to Pharaoh' (a title taken in Egyptian documents by an earlier vizier to the Pharaoh) in order to bring them to prosperity there through his unlimited power in the land. This also, of course, gives the reason for the inclusion of the chain of events in the Bible.

Pharaoh's invitation (45:16–28)

The happy ending continues with Pharaoh's hospitable and welcoming confirmation of Joseph's invitation, sending the ample gifts which show how much he values Jacob's son. When the cortège reaches Jacob, the brothers give such a foreshortened message that it is hardly surprising that Jacob is 'stunned, for he did not believe them'. Convinced by the procession of gifts, he asks no questions and receives no answers. The foreshortening is deliberate, to keep all the concentration on delight at the recovery of his favourite son.

PRAYER
Lord, keep before my eyes that any success or achievement in which I have a hand comes from you, and is your will, furthering your purposes. Help me to see how I can further your work, always alert to your promptings and your will. Make me a humble and generous instrument of your designs.

52 Israel comes down to Egypt

The remainder of the story combines two different approaches, that of the patriarchal narratives before the story of Joseph, and that of the homogeneous and much more sophisticated story of Joseph itself. Immediately, the former style is evident in the story of the departure of Jacob (46:1–7). Then the list of Jacob's family (verses 8–27) clearly reflects the style and interests of the Priestly writer of the patriarchal narratives, with its familiar concentration on family trees and numbers. The arrival in Egypt and the welcomes from Joseph and from Pharaoh himself (46:28—47:6) return to the breadth and sophistication of the Joseph story.

The renewal of the promise

As Jacob sets out for a foreign land, a reminder is given that his is still the chosen family, destined to become the chosen race. Unlike many of the gods of the region, Jacob's protector is no local deity, but is the special patron of his clan, who will protect that tribe wherever it may be. But the reassurance is necessary as he sets out to leave the territory where hitherto devotion to the God of his fathers has concentrated.

It is highly fitting that at Beersheba he should offer sacrifice to God under the name of 'the God of Isaac', for Beersheba was the special centre of Isaac's residence and activity. The promise here repeated is the same promise which was given to each of the patriarchs, from Abram in Genesis 12 onwards.

Specifically the promise looks forward to two events, Jacob's death, with the promise that Joseph will close his eyes, and—in the more distant future—the return to Canaan. It is therefore both a personal and a tribal return. In view of the concept of death as 'being gathered to the fathers' it was especially important that Jacob should be buried in the ancestral burial plot purchased by Abraham at Hebron. Every nomadic tribe has its tribal centre to which it returns regularly, and for Abraham's tribe this was the Cave of Machpelah. Thither Joseph will bring Jacob's body back with great ceremony.

The promise concerns also a tribal return, looking forward to the return of the people at the Exodus. The future is therefore already well mapped out and safeguarded.

Joseph's welcome and Pharaoh's confirmation

This little section reverts to the style and situation of the Joseph story. The heart of the story was in the great recognition scene, and everything that happens afterwards is somewhat in the nature of the last scene of an opera, great choruses celebrating the inevitable happy consequences of the recognition.

Goshen, the region given by Pharaoh to the Israelites, lies in the east of the Nile Delta. There seems to be no confirmation that the Egyptians 'have a horror of all shepherds' (46:34); the comment may simply explain the separate settlement of these nomads. It is the area where the cities of Pithom and Rameses, which feature in the story of Moses as built by the slave labour of the Hebrews, have been located. Indeed in 47:11 the region is anachronistically named 'the region of Rameses'.

PRAYER

If I speed away on the wings of the dawn,
if I dwell beyond the ocean,
even there your hand will be guiding me,
your right hand holding me fast.

Psalm 139

53 Jacob settles in Egypt

This last section of the Jacob story combines three short pieces. First comes another version of the arrival and settlement of Jacob and his clan in Egypt (verses 1–12). This suggests that the previous section had not existed: Jacob is introduced to Pharaoh and settled on the land as though this were a first meeting of the family with Pharaoh.

The most remarkable element is that Jacob, the nondescript nomad, blesses Pharaoh, the mighty potentate. The two occurrences of the word can be interpreted merely 'greeted' and 'took his leave of' Pharaoh; but the double use of the word in four verses must surely be intended to denote that Jacob, the favoured of God, has a blessing from God to impart to the mighty secular ruler. This becomes a statement of the importance of God's blessing in comparison to worldly position.

Nevertheless, in response to Pharaoh's polite questions, it is still the same old Jacob who appears, morose and wrapped up in his troubles as ever, complaining that his life has been short (a mere 130 years) and hard. He might at least have shown some sign of appreciation of the welcome!

Third comes the sequel to this, the last years of Jacob in Egypt and his death (verses 27–31). Just before his death Jacob causes his favourite son to swear to bury him in the ancestral tomb. This is a most solemn oath, the same as that evoked by the aged Abraham in the last biblical scene of his life. By placing his hand at his father's genitals Joseph swears by his paternity itself, and—by implication—by his own whole line.

Sandwiched between these two is the explanation of Joseph's agrarian policy for the drought (verses 13–26). It seems to explain the situation of land ownership in Egypt in the author's own day (verse 26), all land except temple land being owned by the Crown. This was quite different from the custom in Israel, where the ideal was that every man should own his own vine and fig tree, and where ancestral land was inalienable (remember Naboth's vineyard, 1 Kings 21). The time of formation of the Joseph story seems to have been about the reign of King Solomon, when the king was expanding his own land, and was imposing widespread work-levies, which were so unpopular that they eventually led to the division of the kingdom (1 Kings 12:1–11). This note of Joseph's activity in Egypt would have been particularly relevant in this situation.

Goshen

It is tantalizing to search for links with the settlement of Jacob and his family in Egypt in historical records. They were, of course, obscure nomads, whose arrival would make no direct mark on history. It is possible, but not certain, to associate the entry of the Israelites into Egypt with the period of the domination of the 'Hyksos' (the Egyptian for 'foreign rulers') rulers of the Delta (1820–1550BC). These were chiefly Semitic peoples who either invaded or infiltrated into the eastern part of the Delta and took control of the whole of the region. The movement of Jacob's family could have been part of this infiltration.

The difficulty lies in the uncertainty of the dates given in the Bible, which are intended more schematically than strictly historically. The most solid indication is that Israel is mentioned as being again in the land of Canaan in 1220BC (an inscription of Pharaoh Merneptah). With four centuries for the stay in Egypt and forty years for the wanderings in the desert, this would give an entry date of 1660BC, neatly within the Hyksos period.

PRAYER

Lord, you are the source of all blessings and of all prosperity and stability. Make me thankful for your gifts, especially a home from which to flourish. Make me especially tender towards those who lack a home and family, refugees, wanderers and the homeless in our prosperous society.

54

GENESIS 48

Joseph's sons adopted

There are obvious overlaps in this chapter, quite apart from the fact that Jacob is alive again after his death has been recounted. There are two approaches to Jacob (verses 1 and 8–9), and several different blessings (verses 4, 15–16, 20, 22). This is easily explained by a desire to include all the traditions of Jacob's final blessing, but it does make for bumpy reading. The chapter has two principal themes, stressed by all these originally independent traditions: the link of Israel's future prosperity with the patriarchal tradition, and the position of Ephraim and Manasseh.

The blessings

The foremost theme is the link of blessing on Israel with the patriarchal tradition of which Jacob is now the embodiment. The only grounds for any blessing remains the blessing given by God first to Abraham. The blessing given to Jacob by El Shaddai at Luz (verse 4) repeats almost word for word the blessing given to Abraham by El Shaddai in Genesis 17; the repetition shows the continuity of this original blessing to future generations.

The second lovely blessing (verses 15–16) recalls how Abraham and Isaac walked in God's presence, that is, were continually in harmony and communication with God and under the divine protection. The names, that is the power and value, of the patriarchs are to live on in the teeming tribes of the chosen people. Here for the first time God is called the 'shepherd' of Israel; this pastoral image will remain dear to the biblical tradition and will be used richly throughout the Bible. One need only think of Psalm 23, 'The Lord is my shepherd', the image of God as the true shepherd of Israel in Ezekiel 34 and the Johannine image of Jesus as the good shepherd (John 10:1–18).

The Angel (and 'the Angel of Yahweh' stands for God) is also said to have 'redeemed me from all harm', using the electrifying term, *ga'al*, which will later be used so constantly of God, who redeemed Israel from Egypt and (in Deutero-Isaiah) redeemed Israel from captivity in Babylon. The *go'el* (the noun from the same root) is the member of the close-knit family who will always be there to rescue the stricken member from dire distress ('I know that my Redeemer liveth,' says Job 19:25, 'and from my flesh I shall look on God'). In the New Testament the same term is transferred eventually to Jesus.

The third blessing (verse 20) recalls the first blessing to Abraham in Genesis 12:3, that his name should be used as a blessing. That is, his prosperity should be a standard for others, so that there could be no better blessing than to wish the person blessed to be like Abraham, or in this case Ephraim and Manasseh.

Finally the fourth blessing tacked on (verse 22) refers to the acquisition of the town or district of Shechem. The name means 'shoulder' and makes a pun possible, since the shoulder was a special joint of meat, given to the most honoured person (for example, Saul in 1 Samuel 9:23–24). The town seems to have been won from the Amorites by force by Jacob's descendants in the time of the Judges.

Ephraim and Manasseh

The story of Jacob's blessing also explains why Ephraim and Manasseh, not originally among the twelve 'sons of Jacob' took their place among the twelve tribes. Their rights were also rendered dubious by their birth in Egypt of an Egyptian mother. But their inheritance and position are assured because Jacob adopted them by placing them on his knees, though they still also remained sons of Joseph.

One special element in the story is to explain why Ephraim, the younger son, achieved the more important position. This must stem from the blessing. It is insistently expressed by Jacob's crossing of his hands, despite their father's careful arrangement. The right hand carries the stronger blessing. This is again an instance (as with Esau and Jacob himself) of God's own choice of the younger. Natural ability, position and achievement mean nothing to God: he places his subjects as he wills. In fact Ephraim becomes the most important tribe in the north, holding a large portion of the hill-country north of Jerusalem.

PRAYER

The Lord is my shepherd, I lack nothing.
In grassy meadows he lets me lie.
By tranquil streams he leads me, to restore my spirit.
Psalm 23

55 The blessings of Jacob (1)

The earlier part of the Old Testament contains various collections of sayings on the tribes. There are also the 'Blessings of Moses' in Deuteronomy 33 and—perhaps the oldest—the 'Song of Deborah' in Judges 5, in which the tribes (not exactly the same tribes as these) are praised or blamed according to their response to the call for help in battle. It is easy to imagine how these little poems about each of the tribes, no doubt originally each independent and reflecting both the history and the current situation of the tribe, would have been passed on in song at tribal gatherings: 'Gather round, sons of Jacob...' (verse 1).

The latest poem seems to be the blessing on Judah, which already reflects the hopes and theology of the monarchy under King David. It is mere convention that these poems are put in the mouth of Jacob, on the grounds that the ancestors of the tribes are his sons. Their imagery, especially the animal imagery, is splendid, and has inspired countless artists, perhaps especially famously Chagall's stained-glass windows in Jerusalem. They also, incidentally, provide fascinating glimpses into the little-known period of the two centuries between the return to Canaan and the establishment of King David's monarchy.

Reuben. As the first-born, the tribe must have had some pre-eminence, which is reflected in the vigorous praise given in this blessing. But the tribe disappears from history; some unknown tragedy must have occurred. Land was theoretically assigned to it in southern Transjordan, but Reuben is not mentioned in the subsequent history of the area. The Song of Deborah shows Reuben shilly-shallying among the sheepfolds and failing to respond; it was a long way from the centre of action in Galilee. The tribal disaster—sad, after the kindly portrait of Reuben in the Joseph story—is here seen as punishment for Reuben's incest.

Simeon and Levi. These two are coupled and condemned together presumably because of their treacherous attack on Shechem (Genesis 34). There is nothing about hamstringing oxen in that story, but this may be an image connected to the sexual overtones of the story. In any case, Simeon soon disappeared, absorbed into the great southern tribe of Judah. No territory was ever assigned to a tribe of Levi, but it later (when the temple liturgy was established) has firm existence as the priestly tribe, managing temple affairs and possessing privileges all over the country.

Judah. The first two verses are tribal sayings, the last two form a blessing. Judah became the mightiest tribe of all, certainly in the south, and produced the royal line of David. This may account for the prominence of Judah in the story of Joseph. The tribal sayings use a typical pun, *yodu* 'they will praise' and *yudah* 'Judah', to characterize the awe in which this tribe was held. The striking sayings about the crouching lion and its prey must refer to some military incident (now forgotten) during the period of the Judges.

Unusually, however, the tribal sayings are augmented by richly allusive blessings: the sceptre and ruler's staff must refer to the kingship, and tribute from the nations again suggests the expansion of David's great empire, briefly the largest power in the Near East. The further blessing holds out the hope of overflowing plenty in a renewal 'in the final days' (as verse 1), when wine is plentiful enough for washing, and the king's physique is described in strongly masculine colours. These are the hopes that will be the stay of the Davidic monarchy as the centre of God's promises for a renewal of the plenty of paradise. They form the background to Jesus' teaching of the fulfilment of the Kingship of God.

REFLECT

A shoot will spring from the stock of Jesse,
a new shoot will grow from his roots.
On him will rest the spirit of the Lord,
the spirit of wisdom and insight,
the spirit of counsel and power,
the spirit of knowledge and fear of the Lord.
Isaiah 11

56 The blessings of Jacob (2)

The 'blessings of Jacob' continue:

Zebulun. This was one of the smaller tribes, but held a prosperous part of the fertile Valley of Jezreel. The Song of Deborah praises Zebulun for its help and courage in battle; but then it was the tribe neighbouring the battle, and so most at risk! The territory does not actually reach to the sea, but 'Sidon on his flank' suggests that the men of this tribe worked as sailors under the Phoenicians.

Issachar. Issachar received as its portion a fertile stretch of Lower Galilee, just west of the Jordan. Today these are upland plains, rich in wheat. But there are several great fortresses of the Egyptians and Canaanites, which presumably kept Issachar under their control. This accounts for the slightly contemptuous image of a submissive beast of burden, the 'strong donkey lying down among the sheepfolds'. They were well fed but passive!

Dan. The small tribe of Dan lay originally west of Jerusalem, between Jerusalem and the coast. It was gradually squeezed by the Philistine expansion from the coast westwards. First Dan replied by producing the renowned strong man Samson, but eventually they had to migrate to the far north of the country. In this blessing the initial line merely puns on the name *dan* with the verb *din* (=govern/pronounce judgment). The rest of the blessing may be a comment on its position in the north, controlling the trade route down the pass from what are now Turkey, Syria and Lebanon. The snake image suggests a small tribe with great wounding power.

Gad. The territory of Gad lay surrounded by strong non-Israelite neighbours, east of the Jordan opposite Jerusalem. It was indeed perpetually harried by those neighbours, no doubt returning the compliment. Thus the pun *gadad* (=to harry) on the name Gad is appropriate.

Asher. The territory of Asher was the fertile coastal plain north of Mount Carmel, now largely devoted to growing cucumbers and melons. The allusion to rich food fits both the location and the name (*asher*=good fortune). But it was territory long held by the Canaanites, and Asher must have been thoroughly subservient to them. This may be what is meant by 'furnish food fit for kings', that is, Canaanite kings. When Deborah called for help from the tribes (Judges 5), Asher remained comfortable beside the sea, not wanting to get involved, although the battle was near.

Naphtali. The charming figure of swift hinds and fawn for Naphtali is not explained by the meaning of the words. But the territory lay in the high mountains of Upper Galilee, west of the Jordan (now along the Lebanese border). The image may be drawn from the deer which no doubt roamed these hills and forests.

Joseph. The 'blessing' on Joseph differs from all the others. It begins with a little verse (22), like the others, characterizing the tribe—or tribes, for presumably 'Joseph' stands here for the two tribes of his sons, Ephraim and Manasseh. This is the only image of a fruitful plant, instead of an animal, like all the others. Then comes a saying of praise at his valour in war (verses 23–24), without any indication of what war this may be. Finally (verses 25–26) a genuine blessing of bountiful fertility, using the lovely figures of irrigating waters, breasts, womb, grain and flowers. This is the only one of the blessings to invoke the divine name, and four are tenderly used, the Mighty One of Jacob, the Rock of Israel, the God of your father, El Shaddai. These tribes straddle the hill-country of the central spine of northern Israel, where the rich olive groves and vines carpet the hills and valleys.

Benjamin. The three-line verse on Benjamin, again using an animal metaphor, concentrates on his untiring prowess as a warrior. The epitome of this was Saul, a man of Benjamin, who led the campaigns which eventually repulsed the encroaching Philistines.

This fascinating patchwork quilt of the tribes, wittily reflecting their human achievements, geographical characteristics and peculiar talents, anchors those features in their origins. In that small country the variety of terrain, valleys, hills, mountains, plains, fertile and barren, open and enclosed, engenders variety of peoples. The neat animal imagery must have provoked many a chuckle, but no animosity. The brothers turned out thus in later history because Jacob, their ancestor, decreed that they should be so.

PRAYER

Lord God, you willed that all people should be different. Help me to appreciate the variety of the people I meet, and to treasure their differences and talents—even with amusement. Help me to realize that we are all your varied and beloved children, brothers and sisters of one another.

57

The end of the patriarchal history

This chapter provides a solemn and fitting conclusion to the patriarchal narrative in three ways. Firstly Jacob's dying words link back to the land of Canaan and to the story of three generations of patriarchs in which it has been expressed. The family tomb at Hebron is to be the memorial to the whole process of the revelation and fulfilment of the promise of the 'God of the fathers'. This is, anyway, the function of the family centre of a nomadic clan, to preserve and record its continuity. The burial of Jacob too in the family tomb ensures that his clan will not put down permanent roots in Egypt. It looks forward, then, to the eventual return to Canaan at the Exodus.

It seems at first sight strange that Jacob should have been embalmed. Nomads were (and are) perfectly capable of taking their dead back to the family centre without such niceties. The Egyptian custom of embalming is really a pagan practice to ensure that the dead are in a fit and dignified state for their life in the other world. Royalty and noblemen were provided in their tombs (as may be seen in the British Museum) with miniature replicas of all they could need for the future life, food, cooks, servants, soldiers, furniture, even boats for the Nile of the underworld. In Jacob's case there is no hint of religious overtones; it is simply an expression of reverence.

Secondly, there is a wonderful contrast between the almost furtive, and certainly undignified, way in which the hunger-stricken nomads arrived in Egypt and the magnificent court procession which takes Jacob back to Canaan. The ritual of embalming, the period of mourning, the universal participation in the procession, all bespeak the honour paid to Joseph, his father, and their family.

Thirdly, now at last comes the final resolution of the brothers' treatment of Joseph. Never before have they owned up to their evil behaviour and sought Joseph's forgiveness. There can be no real reconciliation without admission of fault. Without that there has remained a continual feeling of tension and unreality, which is at last resolved by the cleansing reconciliation. The subject has never been properly aired, and it is not surprising that they continued to fear an act of vengeance from their all-powerful brother. Despite his tears of affection on four occasions in the course of the narrative, Joseph refuses to go all soft about the matter. He makes no bones about 'the evil you planned to do me', but lifts the whole affair onto the theological level of the ultimate plan of God in bringing them to Egypt for survival.

Where was Jacob buried?

The double mention of Transjordan (verses 10 and 11) suggests that there was another tradition that Jacob was buried there rather than at Hebron. This has been attributed to the Priestly writer. The two places named have not been identified. Goren ha-Atad means 'threshing floor of brambles' (an odd contradiction, for a threshing floor should be open and smooth). Abel-Mizraim, explained as 'mourning of the Egyptians' (*ebel-mizraim*), really means 'pasture of the Egyptians'. The tradition is included, but all the stress lies on the return to Canaan, in readiness for the next act of God's drama.

PRAYER

Lord God, we have followed the first revelation of your loving promise to Abraham and his family, your covenant with them and your unfailing care for them. Grant me the unfailing trust in you which they showed in all their changes of fortune, that I may come to the fulfilment of your promise in Christ.

Bibliography

Speiser, E.A., *Genesis*, Anchor Bible, 1964

Vawter, Bruce, *On Genesis*, 1977—a full and readable commentary, not less scientific than Speiser and von Rad, but more digestible.

von Rad, Gerard, *Genesis*, Old Testament Library, 1956, (ET, 1961)

Westermann, Claus, *Genesis, a Practical Commentary*, 1988—a condensed version of a great three-volume commentary, highly scientific, but reasonably simple to read.

NOTES

NOTES

NOTES

NOTES

THE PEOPLE'S BIBLE COMMENTARY VOUCHER SCHEME

The People's Bible Commentary (PBC) provides a range of readable, accessible commentaries. These will grow into a library that will eventually cover the whole Bible.

A voucher is printed on the last page of each People's Bible Commentary Volume (as above). These vouchers count towards free copies of other volumes in the series.

• 4 purchases of PBC volumes entitle the reader to a further volume (up to the value of £7.99) FREE

• 6 purchases of PBC volumes entitle the reader to a further volume (up to the value of £9.99) FREE

You should find a coupon for the PBC voucher scheme inserted loose with this volume. If for some reason the coupon is missing, please ask at your local bookshop or contact BRF direct to obtain a replacement.

All you need do:

• Cut out the appropriate vouchers from the last page of the PBCs you have purchased and attach them to the coupon.

• Complete your name and address details, and indicate your choice of free entitlement from the list on the coupon.

• Take the coupon to your local Christian Bookshop who will exchange it for your free PBC volume; or send the coupon direct to BRF who will send you your free PBC volume. Please allow 28 days for delivery.

Please note that PBC volumes provided under the voucher scheme are subject to availability. If your first choice is not available, you may be sent your second choice volume.

BRF, Peter's Way, Sandy Lane West, Oxford OX4 5HG
Tel 01865 748227   Fax 01865 773150   Registered Charity No. 233280